First published in 2023 by Hungry Tomato Ltd.
F15, Old Bakery Studios, Blewetts Wharf,
Malpas Road, Truro, Cornwall, TR1 1QH, UK.

Thanks to our creative team:
Senior Editor: Anna Hussey
Graphic Designer: Amy Harvey

A CIP catalog record for this book is available from
the British Library.

ISBN: 978-1-914087-65-3

Printed and bound in China

Discover more at
www.hungrytomato.com
www.mybeetlebooks.com

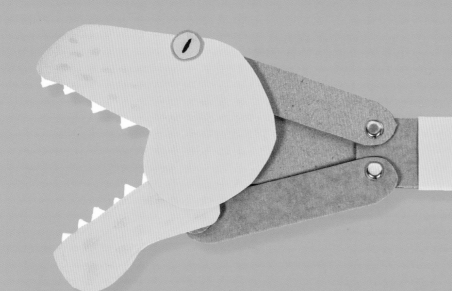

BUILD IT! MAKE IT!

DINOSAURS

BY ROB IVES

CONTENTS

RACING PACHYCEPHALOSAURUS

TERRIFIC CLAY TOROSAURUS

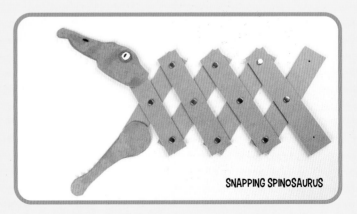

SNAPPING SPINOSAURUS

CIRCLING ANHANGUERA

NODDING DIPLODOCUS

STEGOSAURUS SKELETON

INTRODUCTION

Try your hand at building wonderful dinosaur models! Using smart and simple engineering principles, you can make a whole collection of amazing prehistoric creatures that can run, snap, fly, hover, and more! Each project also comes with fun facts about the real-life prehistoric beasts that they are based on.

THIS BOOK IS INTERACTIVE!

Some of the projects in this book come with templates to help you cut pieces to the right shape and size. Use a smartphone to scan the QR code at the beginning of the project to access a downloadable template that you can print out.

You will find QR codes at the end of some projects, too. These will direct you to videos of the moving dinosaur models in action!

You can also find all templates and videos at:
www.mybeetlebooks.com/build-it-dinosaurs

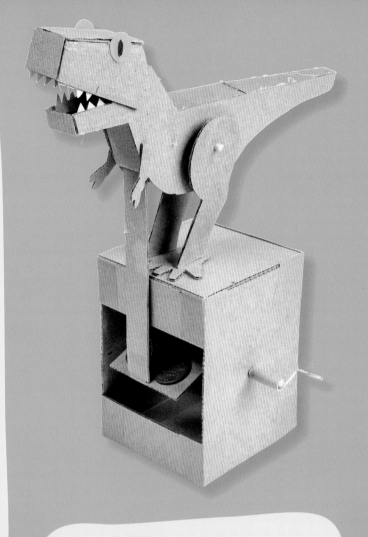

TOP TIPS

- Before you start on any project, read the step-by-steps all the way through to get an idea of what you are aiming for. The pictures show what the steps tell you to do.

- Use a cutting mat, or similar surface, for cutting lengths of craft sticks, skewers, and anything else you may need.

- Use the sharp end of a pencil to make small holes in cardboard (see page 10 for method) or ask an adult to help, using either scissors or a craft knife.

- Use a pair of pliers to help straighten out and shape paper clips.

- Where strong glue is required, you may want to use a hot glue gun. Make sure you ask permission, and do not use it without an adult present. Strong liquid glue, such as wood or epoxy glue, will work well, too.

 **EASY**

 **MEDIUM**

 **HARDER**

These icons are a guide to the difficulty level of each project. They show you when you may need another pair of hands. You will find these icons at the top of the page, near the title of each project.

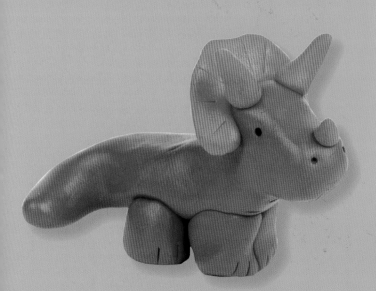

SAFETY FIRST

Be careful and use good sense when making these models. They are easy to understand but will require some cutting, drilling, gluing, and other awkward tasks that you may need some help with from an adult.

Watch out for this sign throughout the book. You may need help from an adult when completing these tasks.

Pressing a pencil point through cardboard and into an eraser, like this, is a safe and easy way to make holes.

DISCLAIMER

The author, publisher, and bookseller cannot take responsibility for your safety. When you make and try out the projects, you do so at your own risk. Look out for the safety warning symbol (shown above) given throughout the book and call on adult assistance when you are cutting materials or using a craft knife, pair of pliers, drill, or hot glue.

TOOL KIT

Every project includes a list of everything you will need to build it. Most of the items you will need can be found around your home, or are readily available or inexpensive to buy from your local hardware or general-purpose store, or online.

TOOLS:

- Pair of compasses
- Pencil and pens
- Ruler
- Craft knife
- Strong glue
- School glue (PVA)
- Craft drill
- Pair of needle-nose pliers
- Wire cutters
- Pair of scissors
- A pair of heavy duty scissors/ side-cutting pliers
- Eraser
- Chopstick (or similar)
- Mixing bowl
- Baking pan or tray
- Cutting mat

NODDING DIPLODOCUS

(DIP-low-DOCK-us)

This friendly dinosaur moves with the help of a swinging pendulum, using a coin for a weight. The best thing is it will always agree with you!

WHAT YOU NEED:
- Small plastic beverage bottle
- Cardboard
- Plastic lollipop stick
- Regular paper clip (about 1 inch/25 mm)
- Paper straw
- Small coin
- Assorted cardstock/card
- White paper
- Felt-tip pens

TOOLS:
- Pair of compasses
- Pencil
- Pair of scissors
- Ruler
- Craft knife
- Strong glue
- Pair of needle-nose pliers
- Wire cutters
- School glue (PVA)

1 With a pair of compasses set to ⅝ inch (15 mm), draw a circle on each side of the bottle.

2 Cut out the two circles.

3 Draw around the lid of the bottle onto a piece of cardboard and then cut it out.

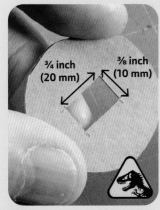

¾ inch (20 mm)   ⅜ inch (10 mm)

4 Cut out a hole in the middle of the cardboard.

You can eat your lollipop now!

5 Cut two ⅜-inch (10 mm) lengths from the end of the lollipop stick. These plastic tubes will be used for the pendulum axle to run through.

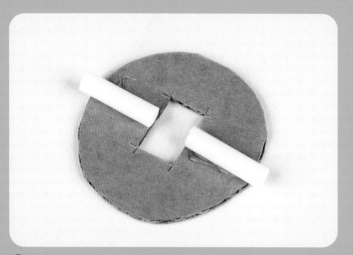

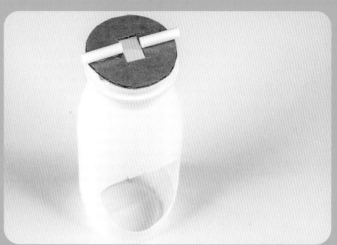

6 Use strong glue to secure the tubes on each side of the rectangular hole.

7 Attach the cardboard disk to the top of the bottle with strong glue.

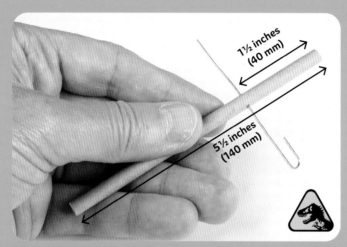

1½ inches (40 mm)

5½ inches (140 mm)

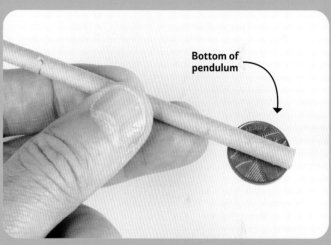

Bottom of pendulum

8 Cut the straw to length. Straighten a paper clip as shown, and make holes in the straw with it, 1½ inches (40 mm) from one end.

9 To make a pendulum, use strong glue to attach the coin to the long end of the straw.

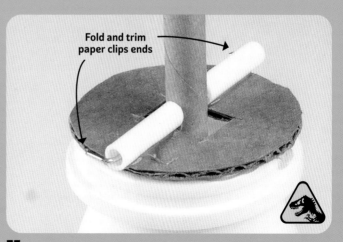

Fold and trim paper clips ends

10 Thread the pendulum into position, through the hole in the bottle, and secure it with the paper clip, as shown. Make sure it swings freely.

11 Fold the ends of the paper clip 90 degrees with pliers so that the paper clip stays in place. Use wire cutters to trim the ends.

Glue on a paper circle for the eye.

13 Use strong glue to attach the dinosaur neck to the top of the straw. Make sure the dinosaur can swing freely.

12 Draw the outline of a Diplodocus head and neck onto cardstock/card, then cut it out. Add markings with felt-tip pens.

14 Cut out some foliage, with slits to fit around the lollipop sticks. Fold the ends and attach them to the cardboard lid, in front of the dinosaur, with school glue.

DID YOU KNOW?

Much like giraffes do today, Diplodocuses would have used their long necks to reach vegetation high up in the trees.

SCAN HERE
TO SEE ME IN ACTION!

NUDGE THE BOTTLE TO MAKE THE DIPLODOCUS SWAY ITS LONG NECK BACK AND FORTH.

HOVERING THALASSODROMEUS

(tha-LASS-oh-DRO-me-us)

Use the QR code to access the template you need.

WHAT YOU NEED:

- Cardboard
- 3 craft sticks
- Small coin
- Thread/thin string

TOOLS:

- Pair of scissors
- Pencil and eraser (to make holes)
- Craft drill
- Strong glue
- Craft knife

The structure of this model creates a clever balancing act, called tensegrity, which makes it appear to defy gravity!

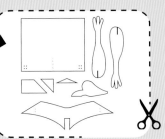

1 Copy or trace the shapes from the template onto cardboard and cut out. Make holes where indicated (see page 10).

2 Drill two holes in the end of two craft sticks.

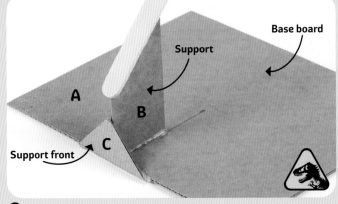

Base board

Support

A

B

C

Support front

3 Cut a slit in the base board (A) (see dotted line on template), and glue the support (B) into it. Then, glue on the support front (C), as shown.

C

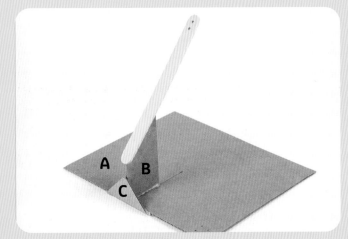

A

B

C

4 Glue the bottom of one of the craft sticks to the angled edge of the support (B).

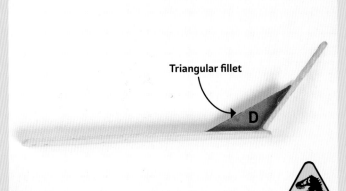

Triangular fillet

D

5 Cut another craft stick in half and glue it to the remaining stick and triangular fillet (D), as shown.

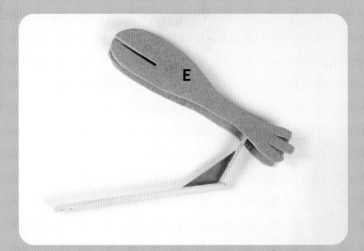

6 Glue the body parts (E) to each side of the half craft stick, as shown.

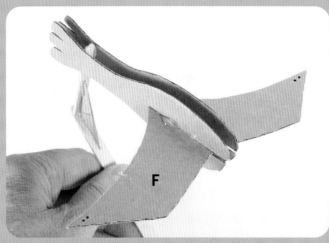

7 Slide the wings (F) into place and secure with a dab of glue.

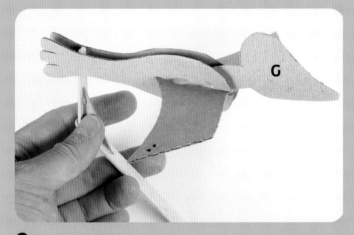

8 Glue the head (G) into place between the two body parts.

9 To act as a counter weight, glue a coin to the inner side of one of the feet.

Tie threads

10 Tie lengths of thread to the wing tips, through the holes.

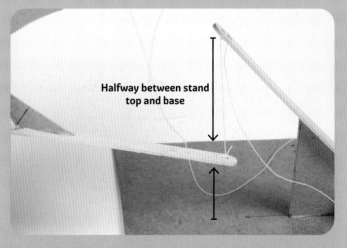

Halfway between stand top and base

11 Tie a piece of thread between the two craft sticks so that, when the thread it taut, the stick attached to the body hangs about halfway between the stand top and the base.

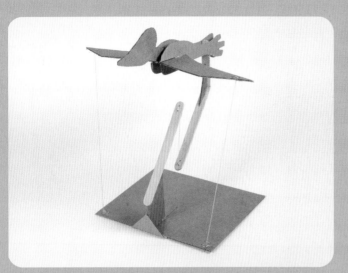

12 Loop the thread attached to the wings through the holes in the front two corners of the base board and pull tight, so that the Thalassodromeus balances.

13 Secure the threads to the base with dabs of glue.

DID YOU KNOW?

Thalassodromeus had one of the largest head crests of any known pterosaur. It is still not known exactly what it was for.

SNAPPING SPINOSAURUS

(SPINE-oh-SORE-us)

Make your friends jump with this scary Spinosaurus grabber.

Use the QR code to access the template you need.

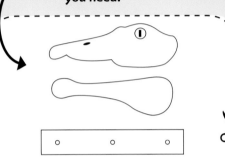

1 Trace the head parts from the template onto cardboard and cut out. Cut out at least eight cardboard strips (6 x 1 inches/ 150 x 25 mm). The more strips, the longer your grabber will be.

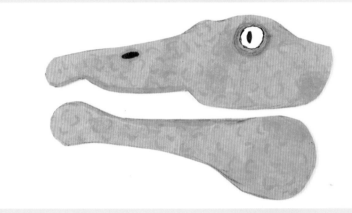

2 Decorate the head pieces with felt-tip pens. Cut out an eye from white cardstock/card and glue it onto the head.

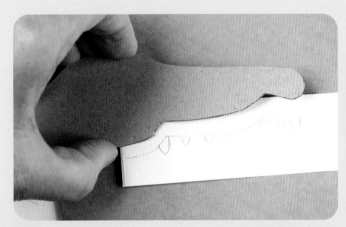

3 Trace around the bottom of the jaw onto white cardstock/card and draw in some teeth.

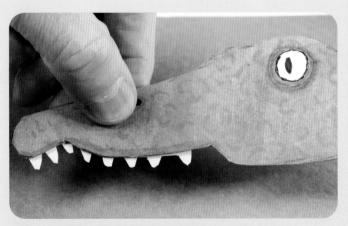

4 Cut them out and glue to the back of the head.

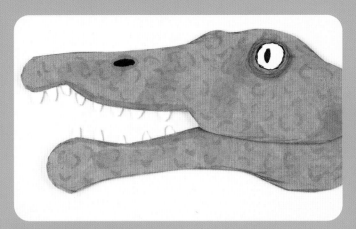

Pressing a pencil point through the cardboard and into an eraser is easier and safer.

5 Repeat steps 3 and 4 to make the teeth for the lower jaw.

6 Make holes in each of the cardboard strips with a pencil. Use the template as a guide for where to punch them.

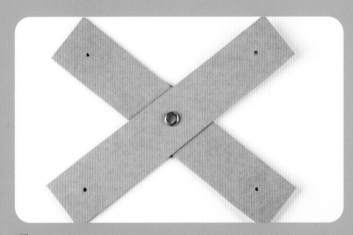

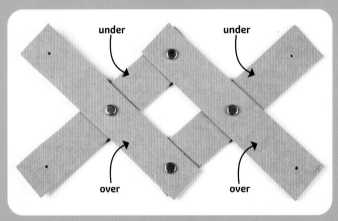

under   under

over   over

7 Thread a paper fastener/split pin through the middle hole of two cardboard strips and fold the legs flat. Make sure that the cardboard parts can move.

8 Add two more strips. Notice the over and under order in the picture.

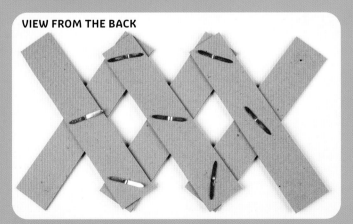

VIEW FROM THE BACK

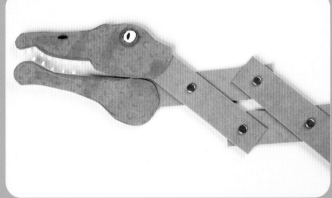

9 Keep going, adding a pair of strips at a time, until it is the length that you want.

10 Extend the grabber and glue the head and lower jaw into place

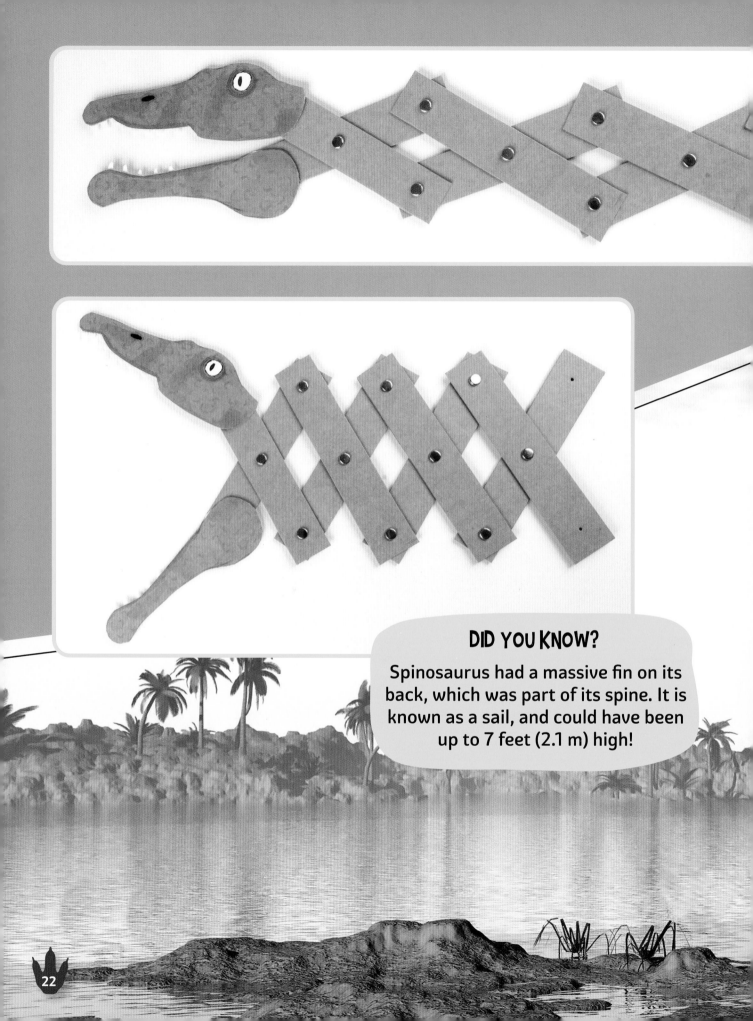

DID YOU KNOW?

Spinosaurus had a massive fin on its back, which was part of its spine. It is known as a sail, and could have been up to 7 feet (2.1 m) high!

SCAN HERE
TO SEE ME IN ACTION!

SQUEEZE THE GRABBER AND MAKE THE SPINOSAURUS SNAP!

23

RACING PACHYCEPHALOSAURUS

(pack-i-KEF-al-oh-sore-russ)

Use the QR code to access the template you need.

WHAT YOU NEED:

- Thin cardboard
- Felt-tip pens
- 3 jumbo paper clips (about 2 inches/50 mm long)
- Paper cup
- 6 (6mm) glass beads

TOOLS:

- Pair of scissors
- Pair of needle-nose pliers
- School glue (PVA)
- Ruler
- Pencil
- Wire cutters

Get your Pachycephalosaurus racing with a simple turn of a handle. How fast can you make them run?

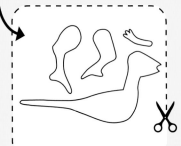

1 Copy or trace the shapes from the template onto thin cardstock/card and cut them out.

2 Use felt-tip pens to decorate the body pieces with suitable markings.

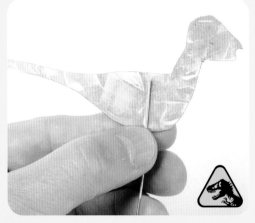

3 Spread a thin layer of glue onto the back of the body. Hold a straightened-out paper clip against it, as shown.

4 Glue the two halves of the body together, with the paper clip in between (it will be removed later).

5 Glue the arms and legs onto both sides.

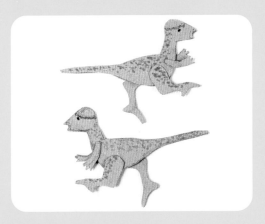

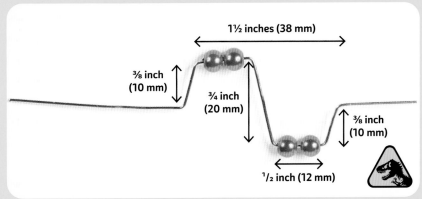

6 Make the second dinosaur in the same way. Once the glue is dry, pull out the paper clips.

7 To make a crank wire, straighten out a jumbo paper clip. Fold it into the shape shown above, using pliers and adding the beads as you do so.

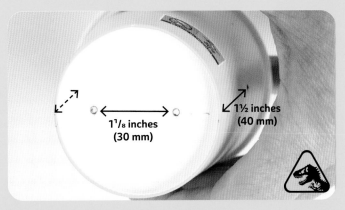

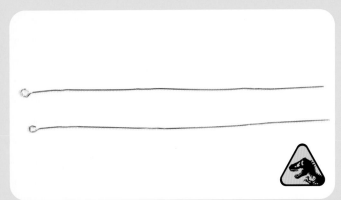

8 Use the point of a pencil to make holes in the bottom of the cup, as shown. Next, 1½ inches (40 mm) up from the base, make two holes on opposite sides of the cup that line up with the holes in the base.

9 Straighten out the two remaining jumbo paper clips. Bend a small loop into the end of each wire using the pliers.

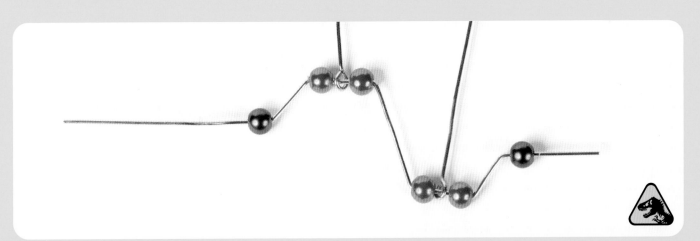

10 Thread the loops onto the crank wire between the two pairs of beads, and pinch closed, so they cannot fall off. Thread the remaining beads onto each end of the wire.

25

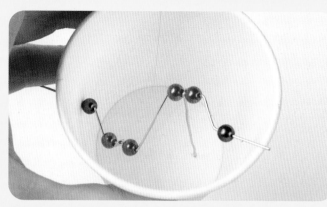

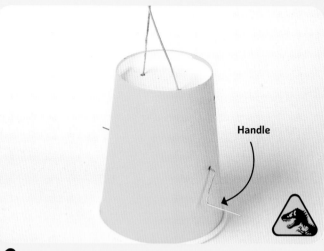

Handle

11 Thread the long wires through the holes in the bottom of the cup, then thread the crank wire into place through the side holes, long end first.

12 Fold a handle into the long end of the crank wire. Cut the upright wires with wire cutters so that they stick out about 2½ inches (60 mm) from the cup, at their lowest point.

DID YOU KNOW?

Pachycephalosaurus had a thick, skull, like a helmet. Some scientists think they might have used it to butt heads with each other.

TURN THE HANDLE TO MAKE THEM RUN!

SCAN HERE
TO SEE US IN ACTION!

13 Thread the dinosaurs onto the wires through the holes you made earlier with a paper clip.

DIPPING DRYOSAURUS
(dry-oh-SORE-us)

Dryosaurus had stiff tails that helped them with their balance, allowing them to run on two feet at high speeds without falling over.

WHAT YOU NEED:

- Air-dry clay
- 3 regular paper clips (about 1 inch/25 mm)
- 1 jumbo paper clip (about 2 inches/50 mm long)
- Craft cork
- 4 (6mm) glass beads

TOOLS:

- Craft stick
- Pair of needle-nose pliers
- Strong glue
- Wire cutters
- Craft drill
- Pair of scissors

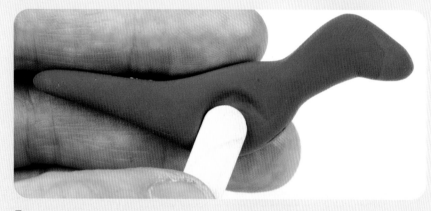

1 Shape the dinosaur body from air-dry clay. Press in the sides where the tops of the legs will fit, using the end of a craft stick. Repeat on the other side.

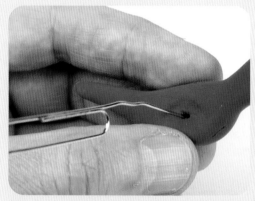

2 Make a hole right through the body with a straightened-out paper clip.

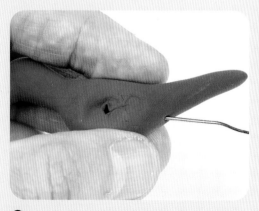

3 Make another hole under the tail for the linkage loop to fit into later.

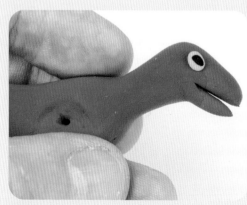

4 Make some eyes from air-dry clay and press them into each side of the head. Form a mouth.

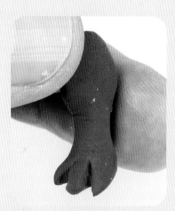

5 Make two legs, one for each side.

28

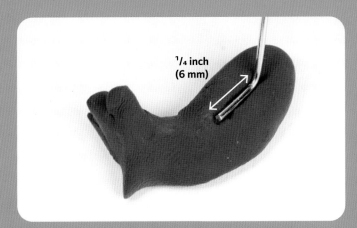

6 Using a paper clip, make a dent in the inner side of each leg, about ¹⁄₄ inch (6 mm) long. The hip wire will mount into this groove.

7 Finish off the body by adding a pair of forearms. Set the dinosaur parts aside until they are set hard.

8 Use a drill to make a hole through the middle of the cork. Keep it as straight as possible.

9 Once the dinosaur has completely dried, thread a length of regular paper clip through the holes in the body. Fold over on both sides as shown and cut with wire cutters so the lengths are ¹⁄₄ inch (6 mm).

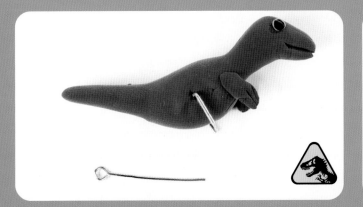

10 Straighten out a regular paper clip and, using pliers, bend a small loop in one end. Cut it to fit in the hole under the tail.

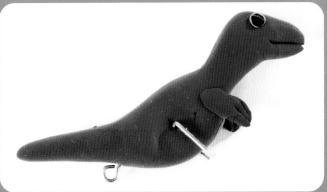

11 Push the wire into the hole under the tail and secure it with a dab of glue.

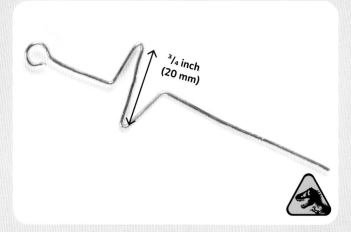

³/₄ inch
(20 mm)

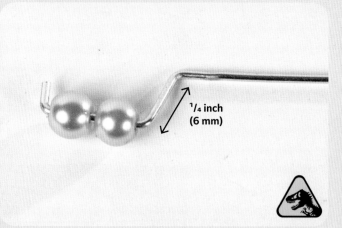

¹/₄ inch
(6 mm)

12 Fold the remaining regular paper clip in a zigzag shape as shown, and bend a loop at the end.

13 Fold the jumbo paper clip as shown and thread on two glass beads.

14 Glue the grooves in the legs to the hip wires. Glue the feet to the top of the cork. Thread another bead onto the long part of what will be the crank wire, and push it through the cork.

15 Thread the final bead onto the other side of the crank wire, then fold the wire into a handle.

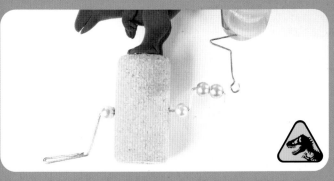

The zigzag in the wire allows you to adjust the length of the pushrod, so that you can get the movement you want.

16 Turn the crank so that the beads are at their highest. Bend the body over so that the dinosaur's head is at its lowest. Fold another loop into the other end of the zigzag wire, so that it lines up with the tail loop and the crank.

17 Fit the zigzag wire into place, between the beads and under the tail.

SCAN HERE
TO SEE ME IN ACTION!

TURN THE HANDLE TO MAKE THE DRYOSAURUS ROCK BACK AND FORTH!

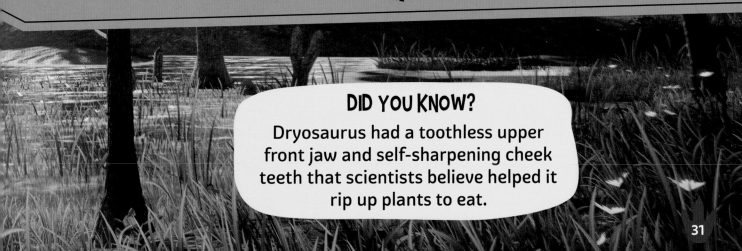

DID YOU KNOW?
Dryosaurus had a toothless upper front jaw and self-sharpening cheek teeth that scientists believe helped it rip up plants to eat.

BENDING BRACHIOSAURUS
(BRAK-ee-oh-sore-us)

Brachiosaurus were massive dinosaurs. They could have weighed as much as four African elephants!

Use the QR code to access the template you need.

WHAT YOU NEED:
- Assorted cardstock/card
- Felt-tip pens
- Regular paper clip (about 1 inch/25 mm)
- Wooden clothespin/peg
- Plastic eyes

TOOLS:
- Pair of scissors
- Pair of needle-nose pliers
- Wire cutters
- School glue (PVA)
- Chopstick (or similar)
- Craft drill

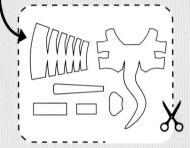

1 Copy or trace the shapes from the template onto thin cardstock/card and cut them out. Decorate with felt-tip pens.

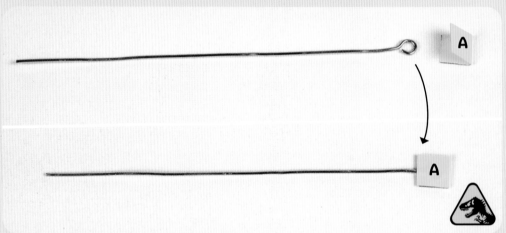

2 Straighten out the paper clip. Add a loop to the end, using a pair of pliers. Fold piece A in half so that it will sandwich the loop on the paper clip. Glue it into place.

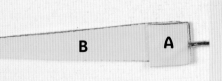

3 Glue the covered loop to the wide end of the pull tab (B).

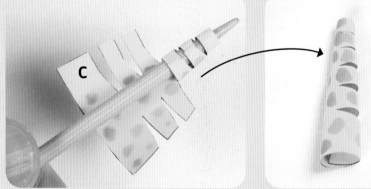

4 Roll each section of the neck (C) around and glue them together. A chopstick works as a useful former for shaping this piece.

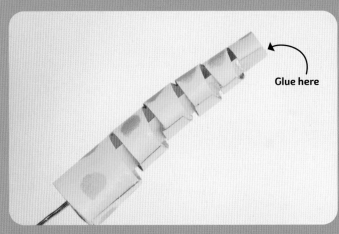

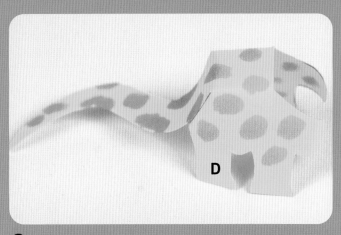

5 Thread the long pull tab up through the neck and glue to the inside of the top section, at the front.

6 Fold the body (D) into shape and glue the edges together.

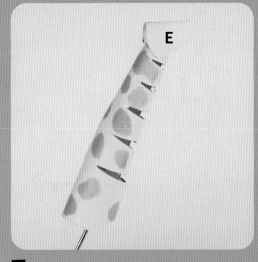

7 Glue the head (E) into place, as shown.

8 Drill a hole right through the end of a clothespin/peg.

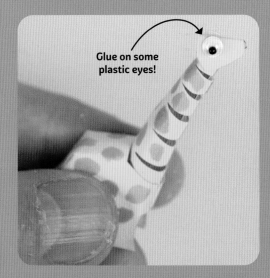

Glue on some plastic eyes!

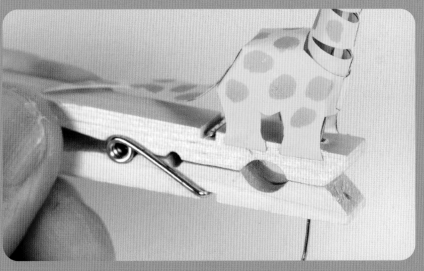

9 Glue the neck inside the body.

10 Thread the wire down through the holes in the clothespin/peg, then glue the feet along the top edge of the clothespin/peg.

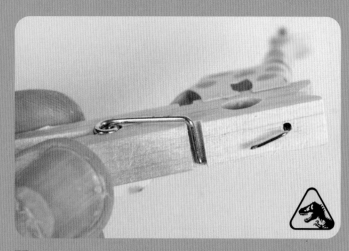

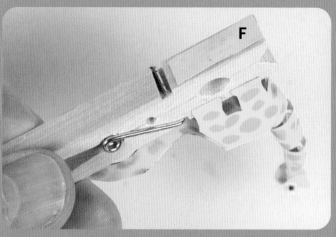

F

11 With the neck upright, bend over the wire and use wire cutters to snip off the excess, as shown.

12 Glue the rectangle of cardstock/card (F) over the wire to secure it into position.

DID YOU KNOW?

Brachiosaurus had front legs that were longer than their back ones. This may have made it easier for them to reach the leaves on tall trees.

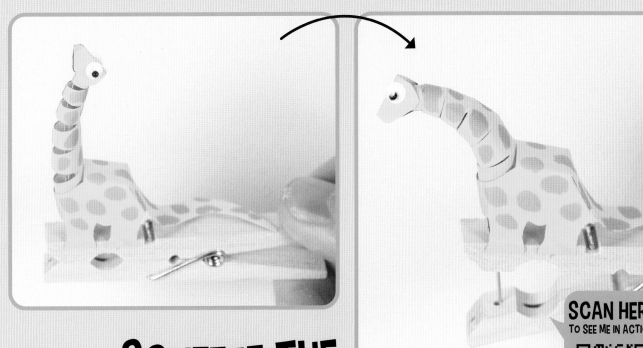

SCAN HERE
TO SEE ME IN ACTION!

SQUEEZE THE CLOTHESPIN OR PEG TO MAKE BRACHIOSAURUS REACH DOWN WITH ITS LONG NECK!

RUNNING COMPSOGNATHUS

(Komp-sog-NATH-us)

WHAT YOU NEED:

- Cardboard
- 4 mini paper fasteners/split pins
- Felt-tip pens
- 2 craft sticks
- Jumbo paper clip (about 2 inches/ 50 mm)
- 3 (6mm) glass beads
- 3 cable ties
- A small jar
- Plastic eyes

TOOLS:

- Pair of needle-nose pliers
- Strong glue
- School glue (PVA)
- Craft drill
- Pair of scissors

Compsognathus were very speedy little dinosaurs. It's thought that they could run up to 40 miles per hour!

Use the QR code to access the template you need.

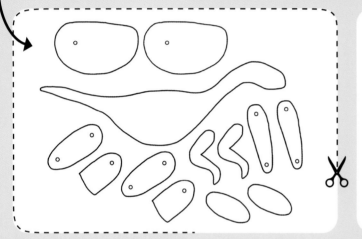

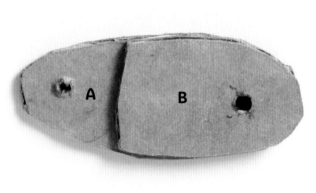

1 Copy or trace the shapes from the template onto cardboard and cut them out. Mark where to make holes.

2 Make holes in the leg and body sections (see page 10). Use school glue to join the upper leg sections (A and B) together.

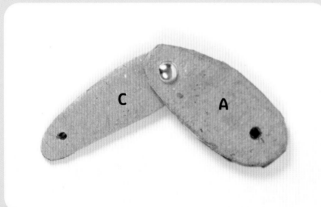

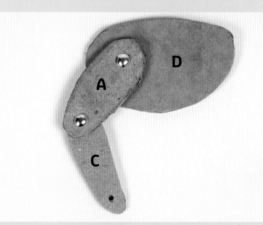

3 Use a paper fastener/split pin to join a lower leg section (C) to an upper leg (A).

4 Join the leg to the side of a body piece (D), using a paper fastener/split pin.

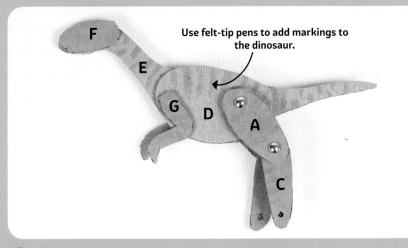

Use felt-tip pens to add markings to the dinosaur.

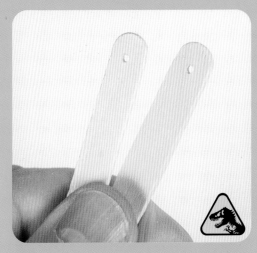

5 Repeat the steps 3 and 4 for the other leg, then glue both body sides (D) to the main body (E). Glue on the head sides (F) and front arms (G), too.

6 Drill holes in the ends of the craft sticks.

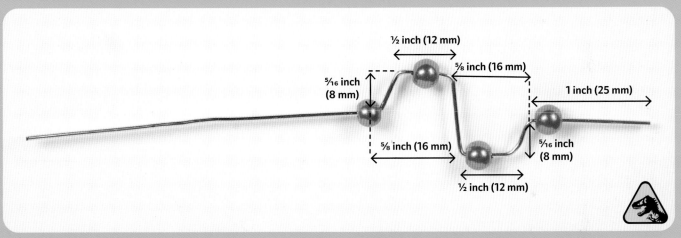

½ inch (12 mm)

⁵⁄₈ inch (16 mm)

⁵⁄₁₆ inch (8 mm)

1 inch (25 mm)

⁵⁄₈ inch (16 mm)

⁵⁄₁₆ inch (8 mm)

½ inch (12 mm)

7 Straighten the jumbo paper clip, then shape it as shown, using a pair of pliers and adding the glass beads as you go. This will be the crank wire.

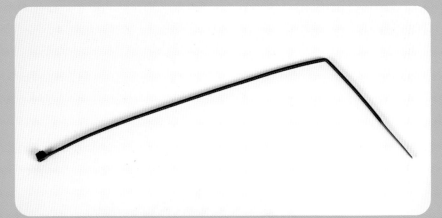

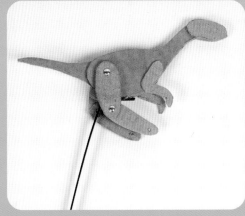

8 Make a bend in the cable tie. It will act as a spring mount for the dinosaur body.

9 Use strong glue to attach the cable tie to the dinosaur's belly. Snip off any excess from the top.

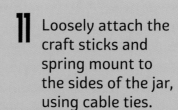

Handle

10 Thread the legs onto the crank (you will need to rearrange some of the beads to do this). Then thread the craft sticks onto each end.

11 Loosely attach the craft sticks and spring mount to the sides of the jar, using cable ties.

12 Shape the end of the crank wire into a crank handle.

DID YOU KNOW?

Compsognathus were tiny dinosaurs, estimated to be the size of a turkey or a big chicken!

Glue on some eyes

13 Adjust the craft sticks and spring mount until the dinosaur runs freely, then pull the cable ties around the jar tight and snip off any excess.

SCAN HERE
TO SEE ME IN ACTION!

TURN THE HANDLE TO MAKE IT RUN!

FLAPPING ARCHAEOPTERYX

(ark-ee-OPT-er-ix)

Use the QR code to access the template you need.

WHAT YOU NEED:

- Cardstock/card
- Felt-tip pens
- 1 each ¼-inch (6 mm) and ⅜-inch (8 mm) paper straws
- Cardboard
- Paper cup
- 2 small coins
- White paper
- Plastic eyes
- Wooden skewer
- Regular paper clip (about 1 inch/25 mm)

TOOLS:

- Pair of scissors
- Ruler
- Pencil
- Pair of compasses
- Strong glue
- School glue (PVA)
- Pair of pliers

Archaeopteryx was a birdlike dinosaur that existed 70 million years before true birds evolved!

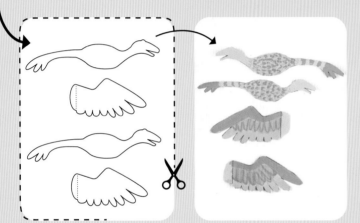

1 Copy or trace the shapes from the template onto cardstock/card, cut them out and decorate with felt-tip pens.

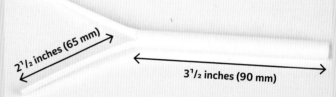

2½ inches (65 mm)

3½ inches (90 mm)

2 Cut the ⅜-inch (8 mm) straw so that it is 6 inches (155 mm) long. Then make four 2½-inch (65 mm) cuts down the straw at equal distances. Cut out two of the long tabs created by the cuts, leaving two wing pushrods.

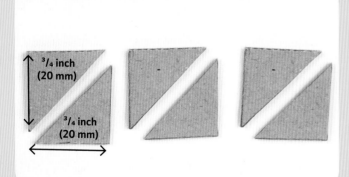

¾ inch (20 mm)

¾ inch (20 mm)

3 Cut out three cardboard squares, ¾ x ¾ inches (20 x 20 mm), then cut them in half to make six support triangles (you will have one left over at the end).

4 Make a hole in the bottom of the paper cup with a pencil, so that it is a good fit for the ⅜-inch (8 mm) paper straw.

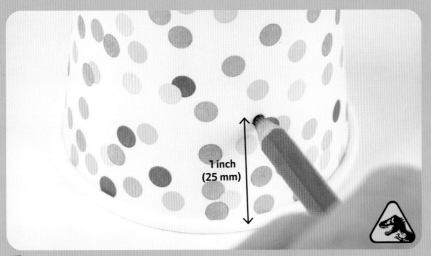

5 Make two holes in the side of the cup, one on each opposite side, so that a wooden skewer can slide through them.

6 Fit the end of the straw through the hole in the cup by no more than ¼ inch (5 mm).

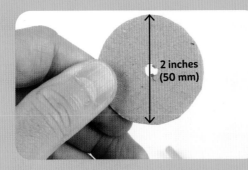

7 Use strong glue to attach two of the support triangles in place.

8 Using a pair of compasses, measure and cut a cardboard circle, 2 inches (50mm) in diameter. Make a hole in the middle to fit a ¼-inch (6 mm) straw (see page 10).

9 Fit the straw into the hole so that it is level with the face of the disk. Secure it with triangle supports and strong glue.

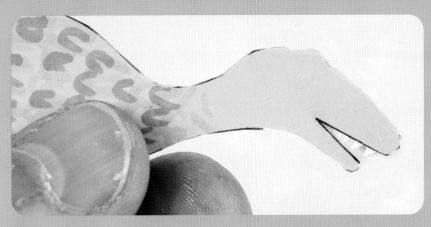

10 Use strong glue to attach two coins into place to act as weights.

11 Make some teeth out of white paper (see steps 3-4 on page 20) and sandwich them between the two parts of the body, using school glue. Glue the tail together with school glue, but leave the middle section of the body unglued.

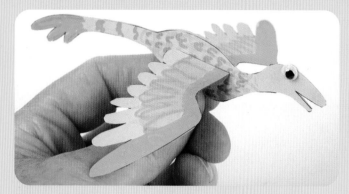

12 Fold down the wing tabs and use school glue to attach them to each side of the body. Add some plastic eyes.

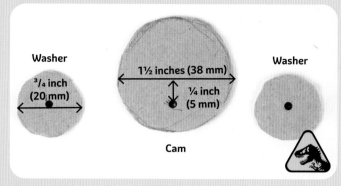

Washer

³/₄ inch (20 mm)

1½ inches (38 mm)

¼ inch (5 mm)

Washer

Cam

13 Make two washers and a cam, using the measurements above. Use the wooden skewer to make a hole in the middle of each washer, and one in the cam ¹/₄ inch (5 mm) from the middle.

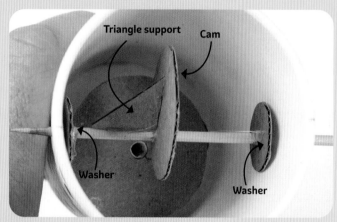

Triangle support

Cam

Washer

Washer

14 Thread the skewer through the side of the cup, the washers, and the cam. Place the cam directly over the hole for the straw and secure with another triangle support. Use strong glue to secure the washers to the skewer at each side of the cup.

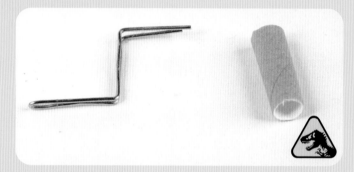

15 Straighten the paper clip, then shape it into a crank handle. Cut off a short section from the ¼-inch (6 mm) straw.

16 Fill the piece of straw with strong glue, push it onto the skewer, then push the crank into the glue. Let the glue set completely. Trim the skewer on the other side of the cup so that only a small amount sticks out.

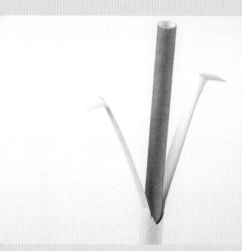

17 Thread the ¼-inch (6 mm) straw through the larger straw. Bend over the ends of the outer straw's tabs. These will work as pushrods to make the wings flap.

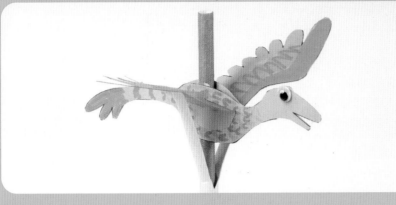

18 Thread the Archaeopteryx onto the inner straw and glue the pushrod tabs to the underside of the wing, using school glue. Adjust the height of the body on the straw until it flaps well, then glue it into place.

19 Trim off any excess straw from the top of the body.

TURN THE HANDLE TO MAKE YOUR ARCHAEOPTERYX FLY!

SCAN HERE
TO SEE ME IN ACTION!

DID YOU KNOW?

The Archaeopteryx was actually small. It was a similar size to a pigeon.

43

CIRCLING ANHANGUERA

(AN-han-GER-a)

This model uses a simple homopolar motor, made from a magnet and a battery, to make two Anhanguera spin around in a circle.

WHAT YOU NEED:

- Assorted cardstock/card
- Felt-tip pens
- Neodymium magnet
- LR44 battery
- Craft cork
- Single core wire (nonmagnetic)

TOOLS:

- Pair of scissors
- Pair of needle-nose pliers
- Strong glue
- Wire cutters

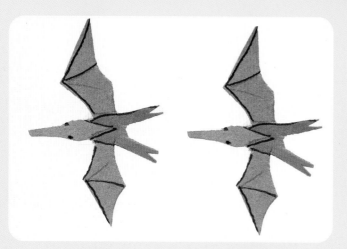

1 Cut out two small Anhanguera shapes from thin cardstock/card. Decorate with felt-tip pens.

Magnet   Battery

2 Put the magnet under the battery, then stand them on top of the cork.

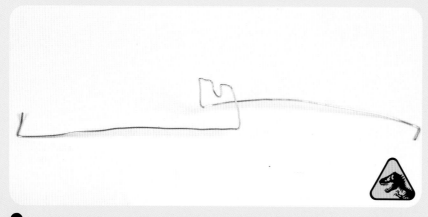

3 Strip the insulation from about 12 inches (300 mm) of the core wire, using wire cutters, and shape it as shown, using a pair of pliers.

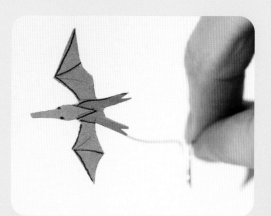

4 Use strong glue to attach one end of the wire to each Anhanguera.

5 Balance the middle of the wire on top of the battery and adjust so that it brushes lightly over the surface of the battery.

SCAN HERE
TO SEE US IN ACTION!

WATCH YOUR ANHANGUERA CIRCLE ELEGANTLY AROUND THE CORK!

DID YOU KNOW?

An Anhanguera's teeth were sharp, long, and curved. They were the perfect tool for hunting fish.

TERRIFIC CLAY TOROSAURUS

(tor-oh-SORE-us)

Its amazing what you can make with just a piece of clay! Once you have made your Torosaurus, why not make him some other dinosaur friends?

WHAT YOU NEED:	TOOLS:
• Oven-bake clay	• Carving tool or wooden skewer

1 Choose two different shades of oven-bake clay. Knead the clay until it is soft and easy to model.

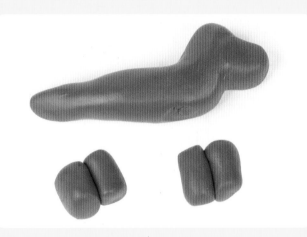

2 Shape a part into a head, body, and tail, then form four cylinders to make two pairs of legs, as shown.

3 Form the legs onto the body. Curve the tail around slightly.

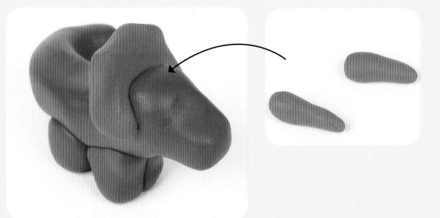

4 Make a crest, using the contrasting clay, and add around the head. Then form two horns for the head and a smaller one for the end of the nose.

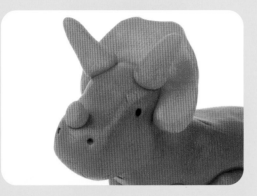

5 Attach the horns. Use a clay carving tool, a wooden skewer, or something similar to add details, such as eyes, nostrils, and toes.

6 Bake the model in the oven, following the time and temperature recommended on the clay's packaging.

DID YOU KNOW?

Torosaurus had one of the largest skulls of any dinosaur, measuring more than 9 feet (2.7 m) long.

SMASHING ANKYLOSAURUS

(an-KIE-loh-sore-us)

Use the QR code to access the template you need.

WHAT YOU NEED:

- Cardboard
- Felt-tip pens
- Plastic eyes
- Craft cork
- 2 jumbo paper clips (about 2 inches/ 50 mm)
- 6mm glass bead
- 4mm glass bead
- Plastic lollipop stick (cut to 1 inch/ 25 mm long)

TOOLS:

- Pair of scissors
- Strong glue
- Craft drill
- Pair of needle-nose pliers
- Wire cutters
- School glue (PVA)

This little Ankylosaurus model, with its swinging tail, is a real corker!

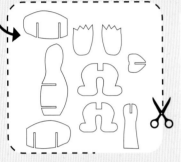

1 Copy or trace the shapes from the template onto cardboard and cut them out.

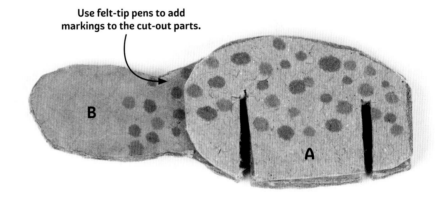

Use felt-tip pens to add markings to the cut-out parts.

2 Use school glue to join the two side pieces (A) to each side of the body (B), so that all the slits line up.

3 Slide the legs (C and D) into place and glue the head pieces (E) onto the body, as shown. Glue on some plastic eyes.

¹/₂ inch (12 mm)

4 Drill a hole right through the cork, ½ inch (12 mm) from one end.

1 inch (25 mm)

¼ inch (5 mm)

5 Straighten out a jumbo paper clip, bend it as shown, using a pair of pliers, and then thread the 4mm bead into place. This will become the crank.

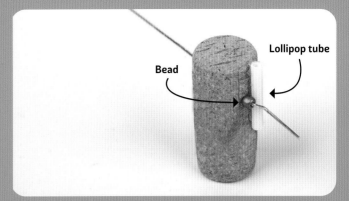

Bead

Lollipop tube

6 Thread the wire through the hole in the cork. Then use strong glue to attach the lollipop tube to the cork, so that it is flush against the bead and lined up with the top of the cork.

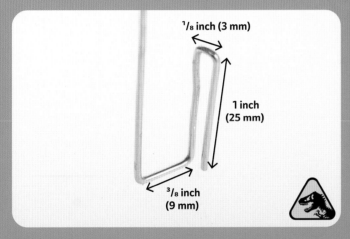

¹/₈ inch (3 mm)

1 inch (25 mm)

³/₈ inch (9 mm)

7 Straighten out the second paper clip and then bend it into shape, as shown.

Crank

8 Thread the wire up through the plastic tube and position the crank into the slot, as shown.

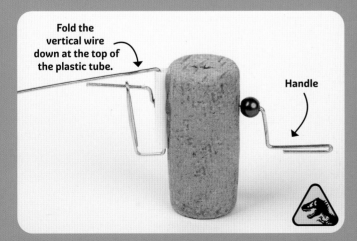

Fold the vertical wire down at the top of the plastic tube.

Handle

9 Thread the 6mm bead onto the other end of the crank, then shape the wire into a handle.

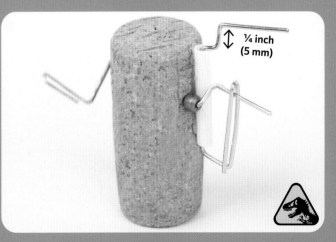

¼ inch (5 mm)

10 Fold the wire above the plastic tube and trim, as shown, using wire cutters.

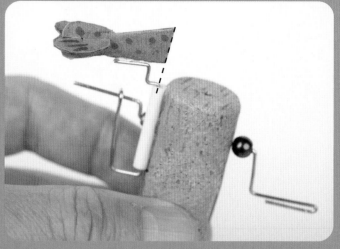

11 Slide together the tail (F) and tail club (G).

12 Glue the tail to the horizontal wire so that the top end of the tail is directly over the plastic tube.

DID YOU KNOW?

Ankylosaurus were thought to defend themselves from predators by using their heavy clublike tail.

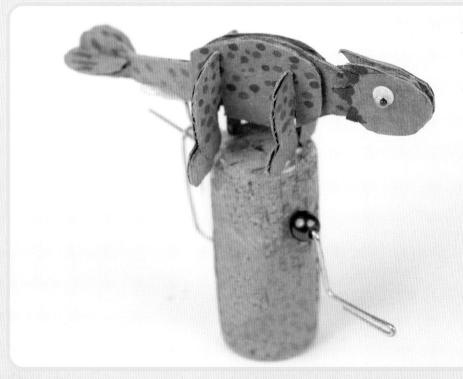

SCAN HERE
TO SEE ME IN ACTION!

13 Complete the model by gluing the feet to the top of the cork.

WATCH THE ANKYLOSAURUS SWING ITS TAIL FROM SIDE TO SIDE!

FUTURISTIC MAMENCHISAURUS

(mah-men-chi-sore-us)

Mamenchisaurus were alive 155–145 million years ago, but this model looks like a robotic creature from the future! You can find electrical connector blocks at most hardware stores.

WHAT YOU NEED:
- Electrical connector block
- 3 jumbo paper clips (about 2 inches/50 mm)
- Barrel-shaped bead
- Plastic eyes

TOOLS:
- Pair of scissors
- Pair of needle-nose pliers
- Wire cutters
- Screwdriver
- Strong glue

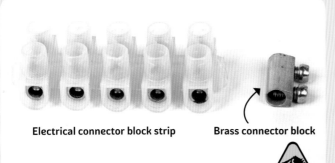

Electrical connector block strip   Brass connector block

1 Carefully cut out one of the brass sections from the connector block strip.

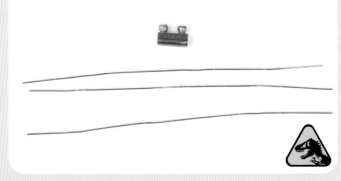

2 Use a pair of pliers to straighten out three jumbo paper clips.

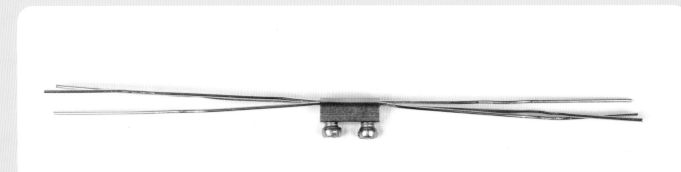

3 Thread the three wires into the connector block. With the wires lined up and the connector block in the middle, tighten up the screws.

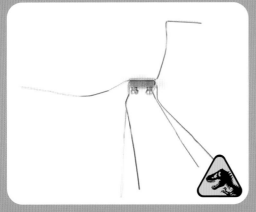

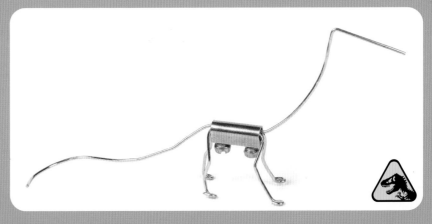

4 Bend down two of the wires to form legs. Shape a tail and neck from the remaining wire.

5 Trim off the legs, using wire cutters, and add small loops to make feet, using the pliers.

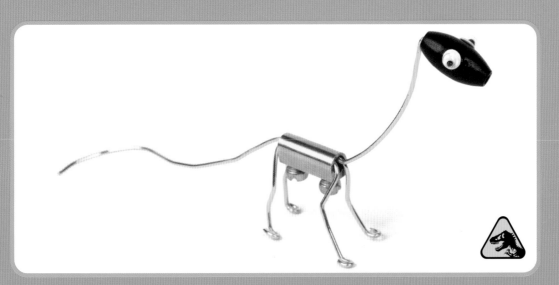

6 Trim the tail and neck to a suitable length, then glue on a bead for the head and add some plastic eyes to complete your dinosaur.

DID YOU KNOW?

Mamenchisaurus had an extremely long neck, which was almost half the total length of its body!

MUNCHING TRICERATOPS
(tri-SERRA-tops)

Use the QR code to access the template you need.

Triceratops had a birdlike beak and a lot of teeth for munching on low growing plants.

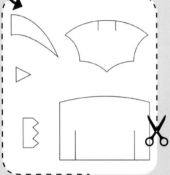

1 Copy or trace the shapes from the template onto sheets of felt and cut them out.

2 Glue the teeth to the lower jaw of a clothespin/peg.

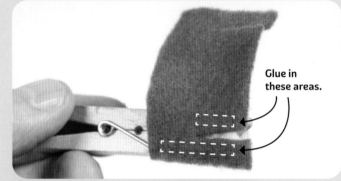

Glue in these areas.

3 Glue the narrow strip of the head felt over the bottom teeth in the marked area, then glue the upper side of the mouth slit to the upper clothespin/peg, as shown. The felt will overhang the end of the clothespin/peg.

4 Roll the felt over and glue it in the same way on the other side the teeth.

5 Fold in and glue the ends of the upper and lower jaws, making a little peak at the nose as you do so.

6 Glue the crest and horns in place, and finish with some plastic eyes.

SCAN HERE
TO SEE ME IN ACTION!

SQUEEZE THE CLOTHESPIN OR PEG TO MAKE THE TRICERATOPS SNAP!

DID YOU KNOW?
Triceratops may have used their three horns to defend themselves from attacks by other dinosaurs, such as Tyrannosaurus.

FLEXIBLE APATOSAURUS

(ah-PAT-oh-sore-us)

Pipe cleaners are great for making flexible little models! Try bending your Apatosaurus into different positions.

WHAT YOU NEED:	TOOLS:
• 5 pipe cleaners (12 inches/ 300mm)	• School glue (PVA)
• A cotton ball	
• Plastic eyes	

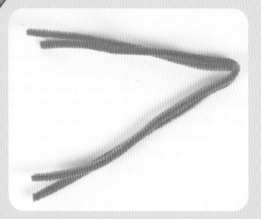

1 Take two pipe cleaners and fold them in half.

2 Twist the pipe cleaners together, then fold a head and neck, as shown.

3 Shape a cotton ball around the end of a new pipe cleaner, to make the body. Hold it against the twisted pipe cleaners, below the neck.

4 Wrap the rest of the pipe cleaner around the body and cotton ball until it is completely covered.

5 Shape another pipe cleaner, as shown, to make the legs. Make another in the same way.

6 Hold the legs up to the body and then wrap the leftover lengths of the pipe cleaner around the body. Repeat the same with the rear legs.

7 Twist the legs and bend them at the knees. Finish off the Apatosaurus by gluing on a pair of plastic eyes.

DID YOU KNOW?

As well as its long kneck, Apatosaurus also had a long, skinny, whiplike tail, which it probably used as a defensive weapon.

FLYING PTERANODON
(TAIR-an-oh-don)

Use the QR code to access the template you need.

WHAT YOU NEED:
- Assorted cardstock/card
- 1 regular paper clip (about 1 inch/25 mm)
- 2 jumbo paper clips (about 2 inches/50 mm)
- 4 (6mm) glass beads

TOOLS:
- Pair of scissors
- School glue (PVA)
- Felt-tip pen
- Pair of needle-nose pliers
- Ruler

Soar to new model-making heights by building your own Pteranodon, with a clever bead-and-wire crank mechanism to make it fly.

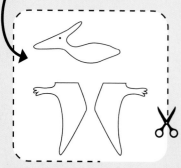

1 Copy or trace the shapes from the template onto thin cardstock/card and cut them out.

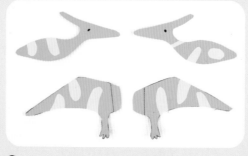

2 Cut out irregular contrasting strips of cardstock/card and glue them to the shapes to make a pattern, then add two eyes with a felt-tip pen.

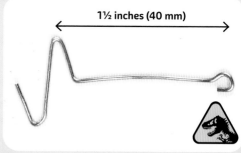

1½ inches (40 mm)

3 Using a pair of pliers, straighten out a regular paper clip and shape it as shown. It will be the support for the body.

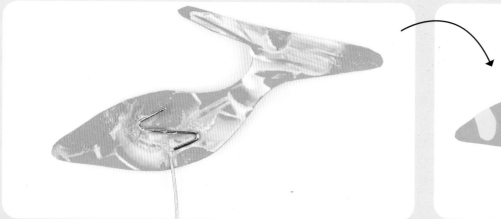

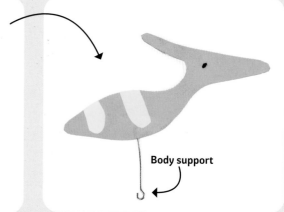

Body support

4 Apply a thin layer of glue onto one side of the body, position the paper clip support, then sandwich it in place with the other side.

5 Use pliers to straighten out the two jumbo paper clips.

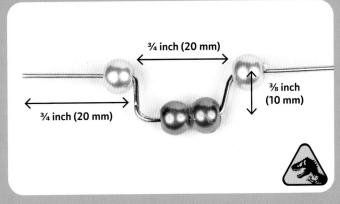

¾ inch (20 mm)

¾ inch (20 mm)

⅜ inch (10 mm)

6 Bend the end of one of the paper clips into the shape above, threading the beads into place as you do so. This will become the crank.

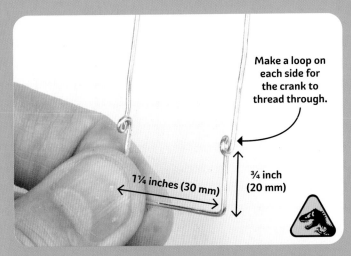

Make a loop on each side for the crank to thread through.

1¼ inches (30 mm)

¾ inch (20 mm)

7 Bend the remaining paper clip into a support, as shown.

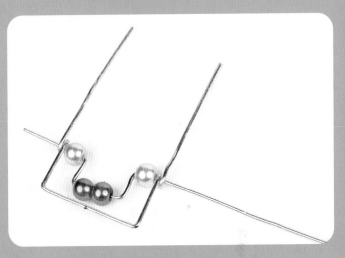

8 Thread the crank into position, long side first.

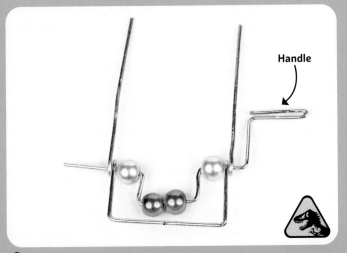

Handle

9 Fold the end of the crank wire into a handle.

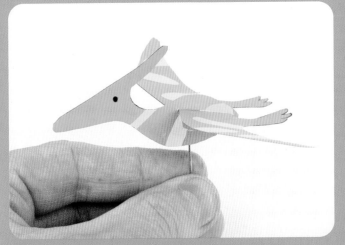

10 Glue the wing tabs onto the body.

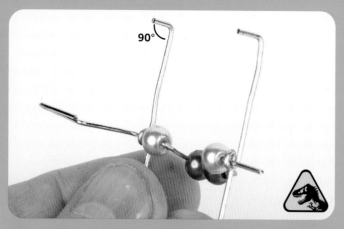

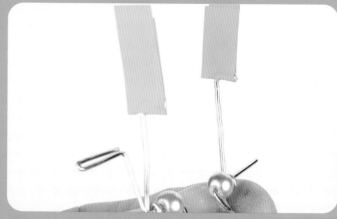

11 Fold over the ends of the stand by 90 degrees.

12 Cut two strips from the cardstock/card you used for the body. Glue them to the top of the stand, as shown.

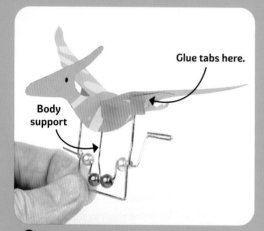

Glue tabs here.

Body support

13 Hook the body support onto the crank, between the middle beads, and pinch the loop shut. Then glue the stand tabs to the underside of the wings and let dry.

SCAN HERE
TO SEE ME IN ACTION!

CRANK THE HANDLE TO MAKE THE PTERANODON FLY!

DID YOU KNOW?

Pteranodons flew over the sea in search of fish to scoop up in their large beaks! They used to fly in massive flocks.

ORIGAMI IGUANODON
(ig-WHA-noh-don)

Origami, the Japanese art of folding paper into decorative shapes and figures, is a fun way to make models! All you need is paper, but it can be awkward to do, so follow the instructions carefully.

WHAT YOU NEED:
· Origami paper
  (6 x 6 inches/150 x 150 mm)

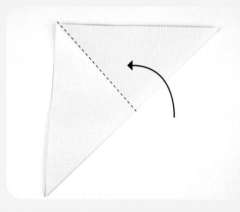

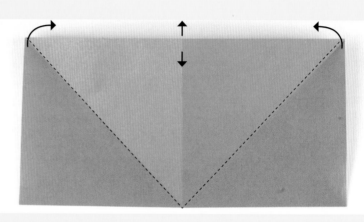

1 Fold the paper in half along both diagonals, with the reverse side facing out. Then unfold it again.

2 Turn the paper over and fold in half along the verticle and horizontal lines. With it folded in half horizontally, pull the middle parts away from each other and lift the outer corners to meet each other.

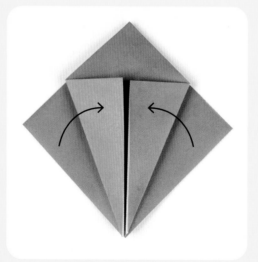

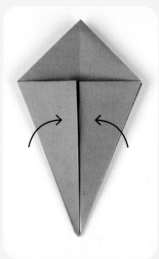

3 Fold down to make a half-sized square.

4 With the closed corner at the top, fold the top edges in to meet in the middle.

5 Flip over and repeat on the back.

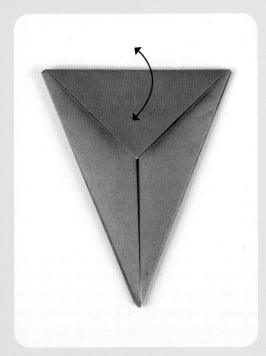

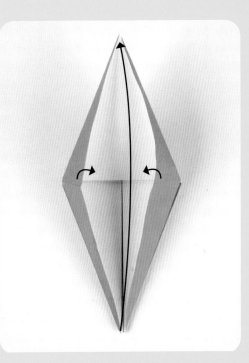

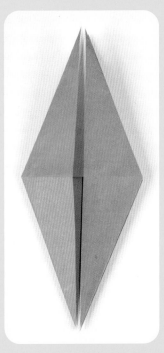

6 Fold down to make a crease, then open back up.

7 Unfold the side flap again. Lift the bottom corner, folding along the newly formed crease, then fold in the sides.

8 Flip over and repeat on the other side.

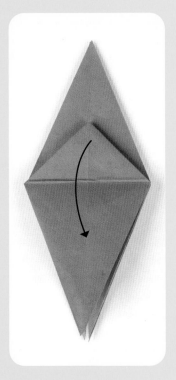

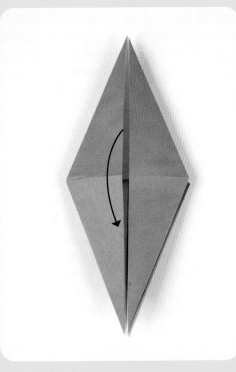

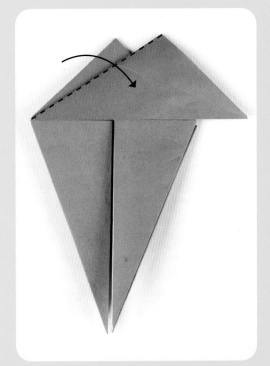

9 Fold down the flap.

10 Flip over and fold down the other flap.

11 Fold the top flap up and across, so its left outer edge lines up with the horizontal crease.

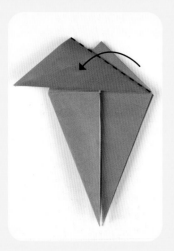

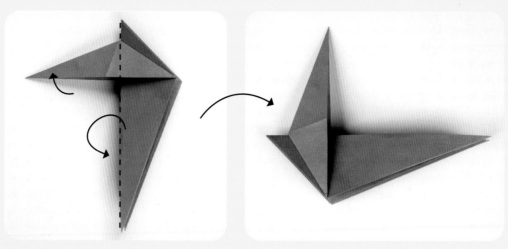

12 Fold the flap back in the other direction.

13 Fold in half down the middle, away from you. Lift the triangle from the previous steps and fold along the creases so it looks like the image above. Then turn it sideways for the next step.

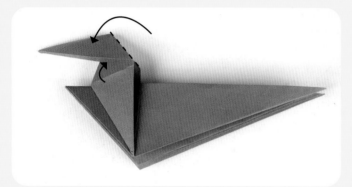

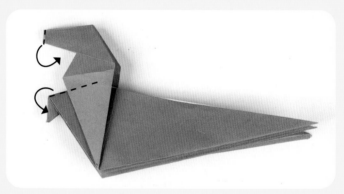

14 To shape the head, fold and unfold along the marked crease. Open out the neck and refold, tucking the neck inside the head.

15 Fold in the nose under the head. Fold down the arm.

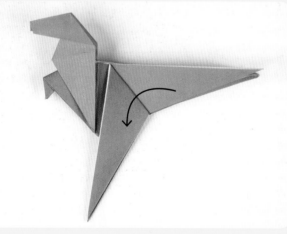

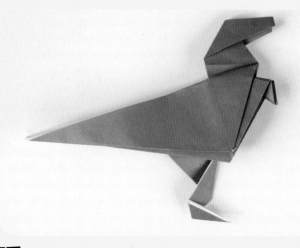

16 Fold down the top of the long triangle to make a leg.

17 Zigzag fold the leg to make a foot. Repeat on the other side to complete the Iguanadon.

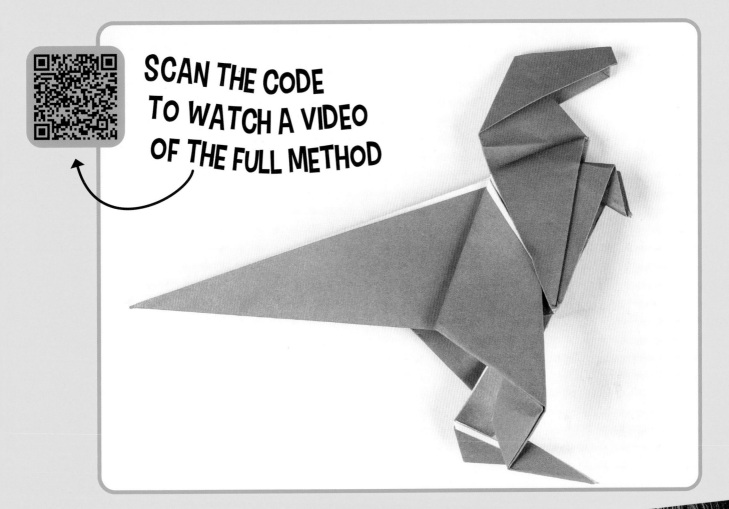

SCAN THE CODE
TO WATCH A VIDEO
OF THE FULL METHOD

DID YOU KNOW?

Iguanodon had spikes on the end of its thumbs. They were probably used to defend against predators.

BITING TYRANNOSAURUS REX

(tie-RAN-oh-sore-us Rex)

Use the QR code to access the template you need.

WHAT YOU NEED:

- Cardboard
- Assorted cardstock/card
- 2 wooden skewers
- 2 small coins
- Paper straw
- Regular paper clip (about 1 inch/25 mm)

TOOLS:

- Pair of scissors
- Pencil
- Pair of compasses
- Pair of needle-
- nose pliers
- Strong glue
- Paper tape
- Craft knife
- Ruler

Tyrannosaurus Rex, or T. rex, was one of the largest ever land predators, growing up to about 40 feet (12 m) in length.

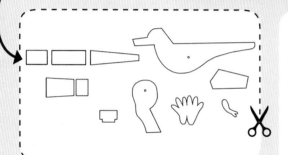

1 Copy or trace the shapes from the template onto cardboard and cut them out. Make holes in the pieces where indicated (see page 10).

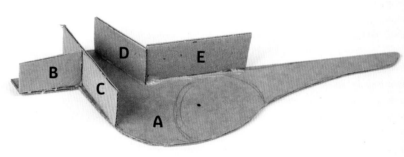

2 Glue the neck (C) and chin (B), as well as the first two body top sections (D and E), onto one side of the body (A), as shown.

3 Glue the second body piece (A) onto the other side.

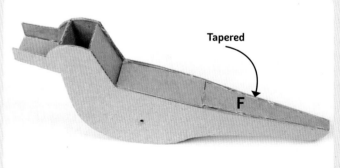

Tapered

4 Glue in the tapered top body section (F) for the tail.

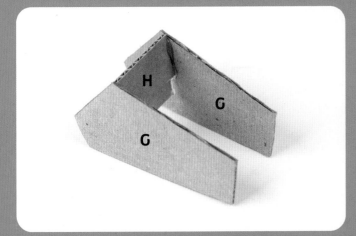

5 Glue the middle support (H) between the two head parts (G).

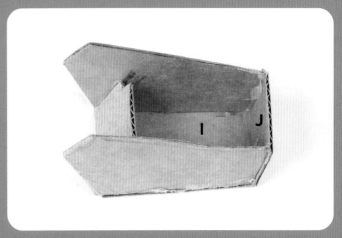

6 Add the top (I) and front (J) head sections.

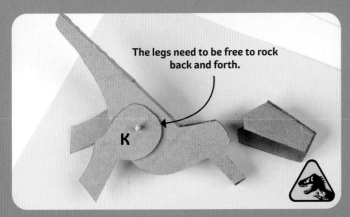

The legs need to be free to rock back and forth.

7 Thread a wooden skewer through the body to hold the legs in position. Trim the skewer so only a small amount sticks out on each side.

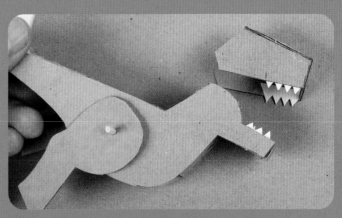

8 Use white cardstock/card to make teeth for the lower and upper jaws.

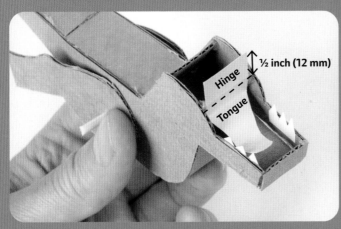

½ inch (12 mm)

Hinge

Tongue

9 Make a combined tongue and hinge from pink cardstock/card. Glue it to the top of the neck piece (C), so that the hinge sticks out above it, as shown.

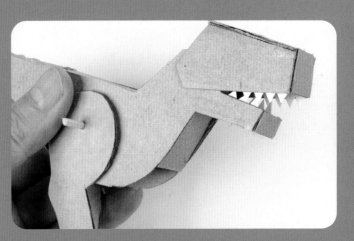

10 Glue the middle support of the upper jaw (H) to the hinge. Make sure the upper part of the head can move freely.

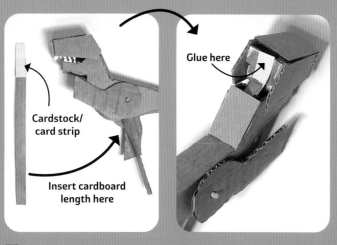

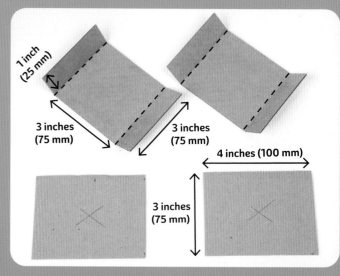

Glue here

Cardstock/
card strip

Insert cardboard
length here

1 inch
(25 mm)

3 inches
(75 mm)

3 inches
(75 mm)

4 inches (100 mm)

3 inches
(75 mm)

11 Cut a length of cardboard ⅝ inch (15 mm) wide and glue a small strip of cardstock/card to the top. Slide it up through the body and glue the strip to the middle head support (H).

12 Make the box parts, as shown above (two of each piece).

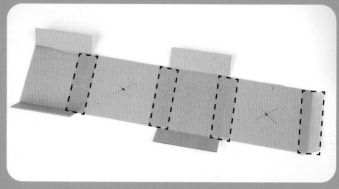

13 Make a hole in the middle of each of the sides (without flaps) with the point of a pencil (see page 10).

14 Use paper tape to join the box parts together, as shown.

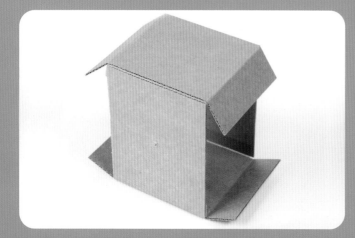

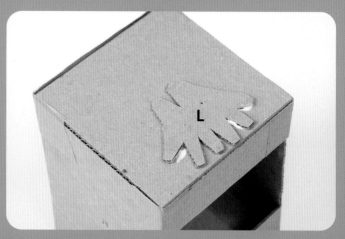

L

15 Assemble so it forms the box shape above, with the two holes on opposite sides. Tape down the flaps.

16 Glue the feet (L) to the top of the box, at the front.

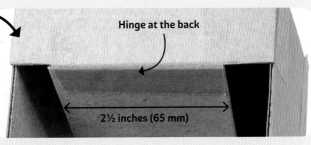

Hinge at the back

2½ inches (65 mm)

17 Cut a strip of cardboard 2½ x 4½ inches (65 x 115 mm), to fit inside the box, as shown. Glue two coins to one end, as weights. Tape the other end to the top edge at the back to form a hinge.

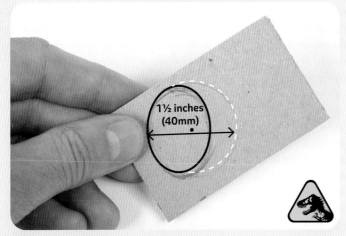

1½ inches (40mm)

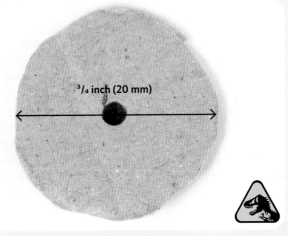

³/₄ inch (20 mm)

18 To make a cam, use a pair of compasses to mark out a circle 1 ½ inches (40 mm) in diameter onto some cardboard. Mark the midpoint, then draw a flattened side, as shown. Cut out the oval shape and make a hole through the midpoint mark.

19 Cut out two smaller circles to use as washers, making a hole through the midpoints.

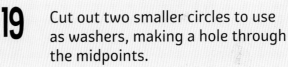

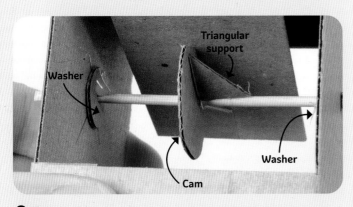

Washer

Triangular support

Washer

Cam

20 Thread a skewer through the box sides, positioning the cam and washers as shown, and glue them in place to the skewer. Cut a small triangular support and glue it between the skewer and the side of the cam.

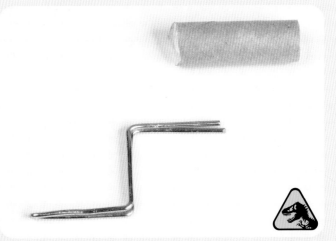

21 Cut a short length of paper straw and shape a handle from a regular paper clip, using a pair of pliers.

69

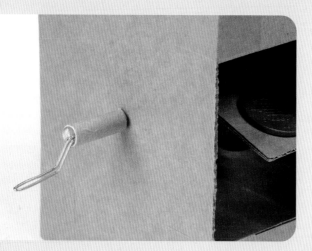

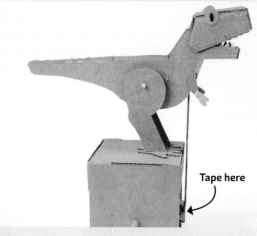

Tape here

22 Fill the straw with strong glue, push it onto the end of the skewer, and insert the handle. Let the glue set completely.

23 Glue the dinosaur's legs onto the feet. Trim the long strip of cardboard, if necessary, and tape it to the front of the flap with the coins. Finish the model with a pair of eyes made from cardstock/card.

DID YOU KNOW?

T. rex had very small arms that were too short to reach its mouth. They were used to attack its prey.

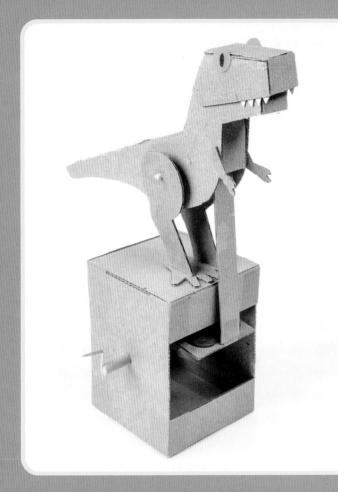

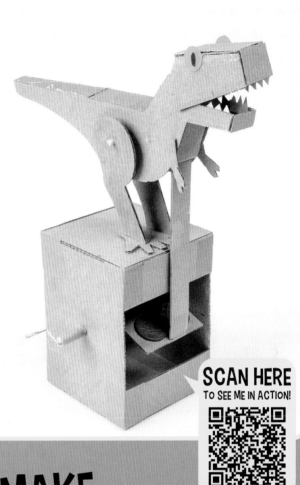

SCAN HERE
TO SEE ME IN ACTION!

TURN THE HANDLE TO MAKE YOUR T. REX TAKE A BITE!

SNEAKY TORVOSAURUS

(tor-voh-SORE-us)

Use the QR code to access the template you need.

WHAT YOU NEED:

- Small box with sliding draw (about 2 x 1½ x ½ inches/ 50 x 35 x 12.5 mm)
- Paper straw
- Assorted cardstock/card
- Assorted paper
- Felt-tip pen

TOOLS:

- Pair of scissors
- Craft knife
- School glue (PVA)

Torvosaurus was scary looking with all those sharp teeth! Impress your friends and family with this smart pop-out version.

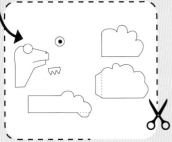

1 Copy or trace the shapes from the template onto bright cardstock/ card, and cut them out.

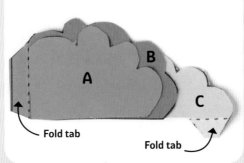

Fold tab

Fold tab

2 Use different shades of green cardstock/card for the foliage. Arrange them as shown, and glue in place. Fold tabs along the dotted lines.

3 For the head, cut along the mouth so the teeth can be positioned as show. Glue the teeth and eye in place and add details with a felt-tip pen.

4 Cut two lengths of paper straw so that they just fit inside the box draw.

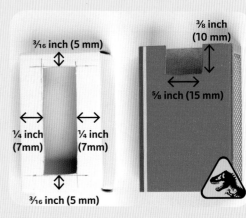

³⁄₁₆ inch (5 mm)

³⁄₈ inch (10 mm)

⅝ inch (15 mm)

¼ inch (7mm)

¼ inch (7mm)

³⁄₁₆ inch (5 mm)

5 Using the measurements above, carefully cut out the hole and notch in the box draw and sleeve.

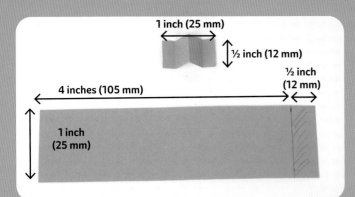

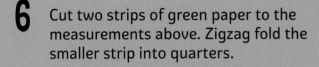

1 inch (25 mm)

½ inch (12 mm)

4 inches (105 mm)

½ inch (12 mm)

1 inch (25 mm)

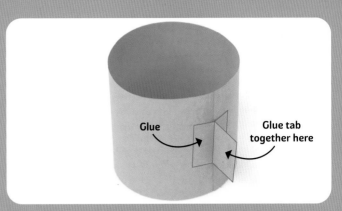

Glue

Glue tab together here

6 Cut two strips of green paper to the measurements above. Zigzag fold the smaller strip into quarters.

7 Roll the larger strip around and glue to make a cylinder. Stick the inner folds of the small strip together, then glue the flaps to the side of the cylinder to make a tab, as shown.

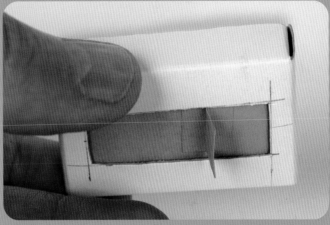

8 Thread the two paper straws through the cylinder and glue them into the box to make a belt. The tab should poke out through the hole in the back of the draw. Be careful not to glue down the paper belt and make sure it is free to move from side to side.

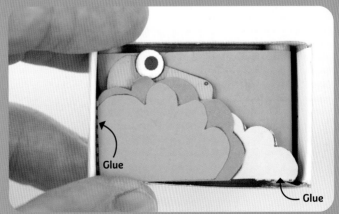

Glue

Glue

9 With the belt tab pushed to the right side of the hole at the back (with the front facing you), glue the head on the far left of the belt.

10 Glue the foliage tabs to the left and bottom sides of the box draw.

DID YOU KNOW?

Torvosaurus could have grown to as long as a school bus and weigh as much as two hippos!

11 Slide on the box sleeve and glue the belt tab to the back, as shown.

SCAN HERE
TO SEE ME IN ACTION!

OPEN AND CLOSE THE BOX TO MAKE THE TORVOSAURUS PEEP OUT.

GROWLING GIGANOTOSAURUS

(jig-an-OH-toe-SORE-us)

Use the QR code to access the template you need.

WHAT YOU NEED:
- Cardboard
- 6 paper fasteners/split pins
- Cardstock/card
- Felt-tip pens

TOOLS:
- Pair of scissors
- Pencil
- School glue (PVA)
- Ruler

Giganotosaurus had a weaker bite than the famous T. rex, but that did not stop it from snapping up its prey!

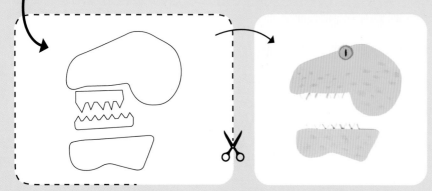

1 Use the template to cut out the dinosaur head lower jaw, and teeth from cardstock/card. Glue on the teeth and eyes in the positions shown, and decorate with felt-tip pens.

2 Cut two strips of cardboard measuring 1¼ x 6 inches (30 x 150 mm), and one strip measuring ¾ x 12 inches (20 x 300 mm).

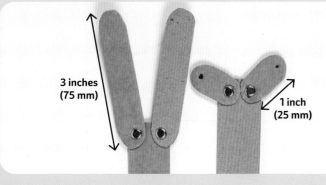

3 inches (75 mm)

1 inch (25 mm)

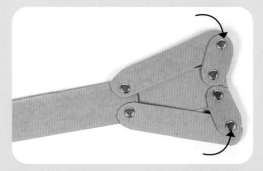

3 Cut two 3-inch (75 mm) pieces, and two 1-inch (25 mm) pieces from the long strip of cardboard to make four linkages. Round off the corners. Join each pair to the end of one of the remaining cardboard strips with paper fasteners/split pins. Make sure they rotate freely.

4 Join the two sets of linkages together with two more paper fasteners/split pins, as shown. The two big cardboard strips should be resting on top of each other.

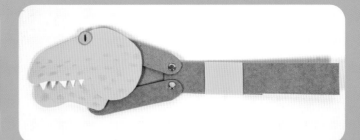

5 Glue the lower jaw to one of the short linkages.

6 In the same way, glue the upper jaw to the other short linkage.

7 Make a sleeve from cardstock/card that is long enough to wrap around both cardboard strips. Glue it to the back strip, fold it around and glue the other end to the back of itself. The upper cardboard strip must be free to slide in the sleeve.

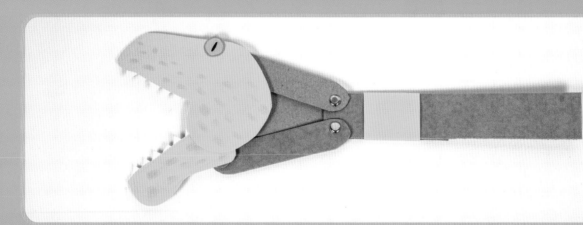

SCAN HERE TO SEE ME IN ACTION!

HOLD THE SLEEVE AND PULL THE UPPER CARDBOARD STRIP TO OPEN WIDE!

DID YOU KNOW?

Giganotosaurus was not the smartest dinosaur, with a brain the size of a banana!

DIMORPHODON PENCIL TOPPER
(die-MOR-foe-don)

Why not make this flapping friend to help you with your homework?

Use the QR code to access the template you need.

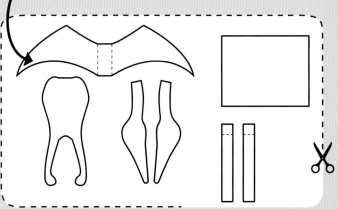

1 Copy or trace the shapes from the template onto thin cardstock/card and cut them out. Draw a face on the head with felt-tip pens.

A

HB

B

Slider

2 Fold over the body (A) and glue it to the end of a pencil. Roll the slider piece (B) around the pencil and glue it to itself. Make sure it is free to slide up and down the pencil.

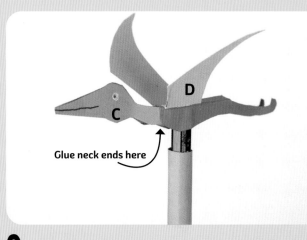

D

C

Glue neck ends here

3 Glue the two head pieces (C) together at the head only, then glue the neck ends into the body. Glue the wings (D) across the back, bending them up at the fold lines.

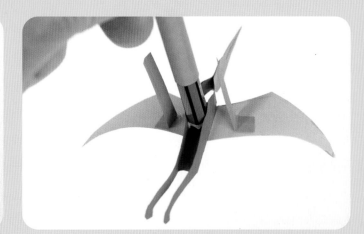

4 Glue the tabs of the pushrods (E) to the bottom of the wings, as shown.

Glue here

MAKE YOUR DIMORPHODON FLY BY MOVING THE SLIDER TUBE UP AND DOWN.

SCAN HERE
TO SEE ME IN ACTION!

5 Glue the other ends of the pushrods to the slider tube.

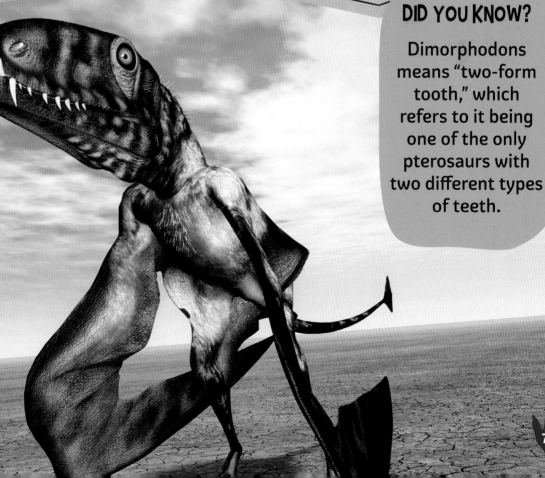

DID YOU KNOW?

Dimorphodons means "two-form tooth," which refers to it being one of the only pterosaurs with two different types of teeth.

PEEPING CAMARASAURUS

(KAM-ar-a-sore-us)

These plant-eating dinosaurs probably lived and moved around in herds.

Use the QR code to access the template you need.

WHAT YOU NEED:
- Cardboard
- 2 paper fasteners/ split pins
- Cardstock/card
- Felt-tip pens

TOOLS:
- Pair of scissors
- School glue (PVA)
- Pencil
- Ruler

1 Copy or trace the shapes from the template onto bright cardstock/ card and then cut them out.

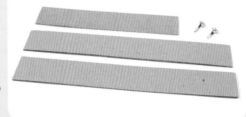

2 Cut two strips of cardboard measuring 1¼ x 6 inches (30 x 150 mm) and one strip measuring 1¼ x 5 inches (30 x 125 mm).

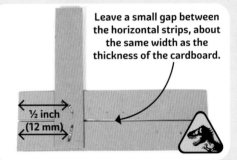

Leave a small gap between the horizontal strips, about the same width as the thickness of the cardboard.

½ inch (12 mm)

3 Join together the three strips using paper fasteners/split pins, as shown. Use the point of a pencil to make the holes for the pins to go through (see page 10).

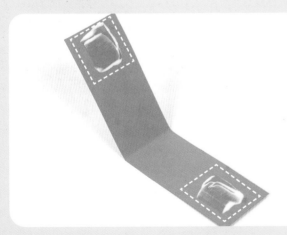

4 Cut a strip of cardstock/card long enough to wrap over both sides of the horizontal bars of cardboard. Add glue to the tips.

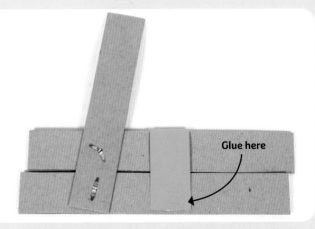

Glue here

5 Fold it around the cardboard and glue it to the lower cardboard bar on both sides, so the upper piece of cardboard can slide freely from side to side.

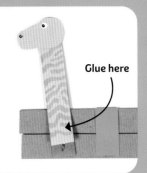

Glue here

6 Decorate your dinosaur's head and neck with felt-tip pens and then glue the pieces to the vertical cardboard bar.

Glue here

7 Cut out some bushes from cardstock/card and glue them together to the lower bar, making sure that the upper bar and dinosaur can move freely.

SCAN HERE
TO SEE ME IN ACTION!

PUSH AND PULL THE UPPER BAR TO MAKE THE CAMARASAURUS PEEP OUT FROM THE BUSHES!

DID YOU KNOW?

The Camarasaurus had hollow chambers in its spine, which made the neck skeleton lighter.

ROARING ALBERTOSAURUS

(al-BERT-oh-saw-russ)

Use the QR code to access the template you need.

WHAT YOU NEED:

- Cardboard (6 x 8 inches/ 150 mm x 200 mm)
- Assorted cardstock/ card
- Felt-tip pens

TOOLS:

- Pair of scissors
- Ruler
- Craft knife
- Pair of compasses
- School glue (PVA)

This fun project would make a great greetings card for a friend! Just write your message on the back.

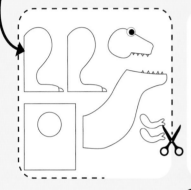

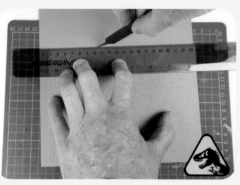

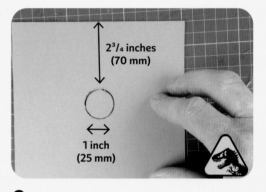

2³/₄ inches (70 mm)

1 inch (25 mm)

1 Copy or trace the shapes from the template onto bright paper and cut them out.

2 Cut some green cardstock/ card the same size as the cardboard (6 x 8 inches/ 150 mm x 200 mm). Glue the card to the cardboard.

3 Use a pair of compasses to measure the circle shown above, and cut it out of the cardboard. Trim the circular piece slightly so that it fits loosely back in the hole.

4 Add suitable markings to your dinosaur pieces with felt-tip pens.

5 Glue the dinosaur parts onto the card as shown. Trim off any of the head that covers the circular hole.

6 Glue the front limbs into position and add the cut-out circle.

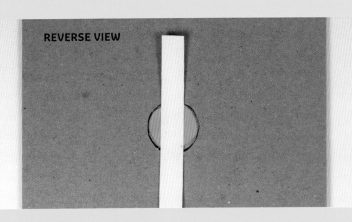

7 Glue the head to the front of the disk. Don't get any glue on the card, so the head can rotate freely.

8 Cut a strip of cardstock/card 4 x 1 inches (100 mm x 25 mm). Fold it in half along its length and glue it together to make a double thickness card. Glue it to the back of the disk, making sure it is still free to turn.

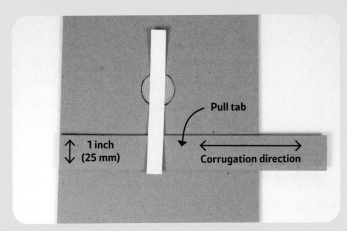

Pull tab

1 inch (25 mm)

Corrugation direction

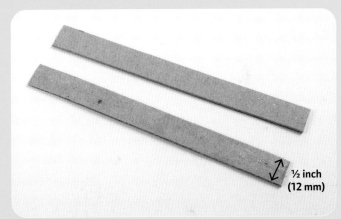

½ inch (12 mm)

9 Cut a strip of cardboard about 1 inch (25 mm) wide. This will be the pull tab that operates the card.

10 Cut two thin strips, ½ inch (12 mm) wide. These will be the guides for the pull tab.

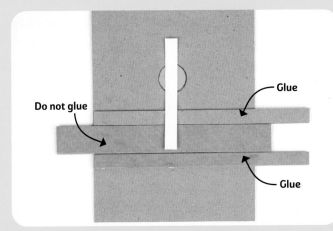

Do not glue

Glue

Glue

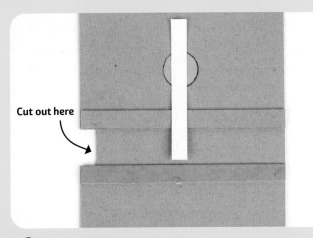

Cut out here

11 Glue the two thin strips to the backboard, leaving the pull tab in between unglued.

12 Temporarily remove the pull tab. Trim off the excess from the thin guide pieces, and cut out a small section between the guides, as shown.

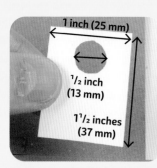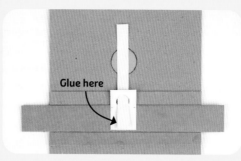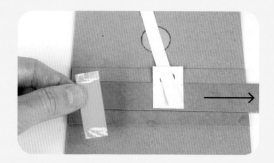

13 Make this link piece from a double thickness of cardstock/card.

14 Replace the pull tab. Thread the link piece onto the vertical arm and glue it to the middle of the pull tab. Move the pull tab from side to side to make sure it is turning the vertical arm.

15 Move the pull tab to the right so the dinosaur's jaw is in the closed position. Cut two ¾-inch (50 mm) stop pieces from thin cardstock/card. Spread glue on each end but not the middle.

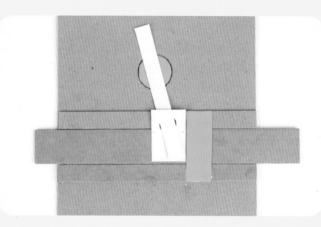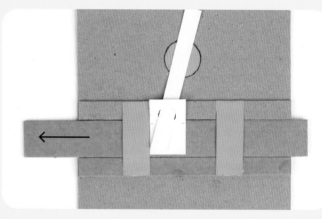

16 Glue one stop up against the link piece, making sure the pull tab can still move freely.

17 Move the pull tab to the other side, so the dinosaur's jaw is open. Glue the other stop on the other side of the link piece.

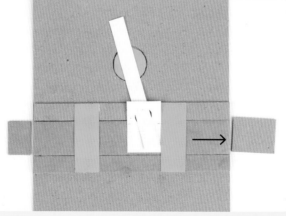

18 With the tab to the right and the jaw closed, trim off the excess from the pull tab.

19 Cut out some leaves from cardstock/card and glue them to the front of the card as decoration.

SCAN HERE
TO SEE ME IN ACTION!

PULL THE TAB TO MAKE THE ALBERTOSAURUS ROAR!

DID YOU KNOW?

Although movies have made us believe that dinosaurs roared, experts now think they would more probably have growled, hissed, or even honked!

FANTASTIC FOSSILS

Why wait millions of years when you could make your own fossils now, using everyday materials from around your home.

1 Collect together a variety of toy dinosaurs.

2 To make a salt dough, add the flour, salt, and water to a bowl.

3 Mix the ingredients with your hands to form a dough.

4 Pull off walnut-sized pieces of dough, roll them into balls, then flatten them on your work surface. Make footprints in the dough with plastic dinosaur feet.

5 You can also press the side of a dinosaur into the dough to make a fossil imprint.

6 Place the dough shapes onto a baking pan or tray and bake in the oven for 3 hours at 230°F (110°C) to make them hard as a rock!

DID YOU KNOW?
Fossils are remains or traces of plants and animals that lived millions of years ago. Without fossils we would have no idea that dinosaurs ever existed!

HATCHING DINO EGG

Use the QR code to access the template you need.

WHAT YOU NEED:
- Thin cardboard
- Cardstock/card
- White paper
- Felt-tip pens

TOOLS:
- Pair of scissors
- School glue (PVA)

As far as we know, all dinosaurs laid eggs. What kind of baby dinosaur will you put inside your surprise hatching egg?

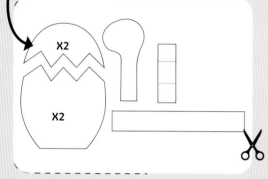

1 Copy or trace the egg pieces twice and a long tab onto thin cardboard, and the dinosaur head and sleeve onto cardstock/card. Cut them out.

2 Glue the dinosaur head to the long tab. Wrap and glue the sleeve around the long tab, so that it slides up and down freely.

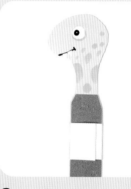

3 Add markings and features to the head, using white paper and felt-tip pens.

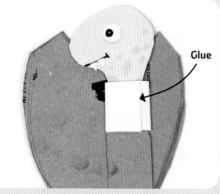

4 Glue the sleeve to the inside of the lower egg shell, so that the head can slide up and down.

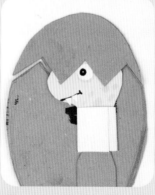

5 Glue both of the upper shells onto the front and back of the head.

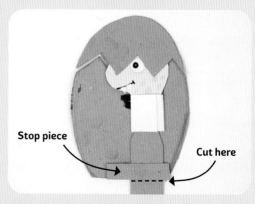

6 Cut a 2 x ½ inch (50 x 12 mm) stop piece from a scrap of cardboard, and glue it to the slider, as shown, to limit how much the egg can open. Cut off the excess slider below the stop.

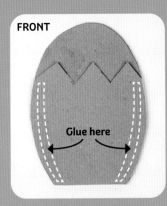

FRONT

Glue here

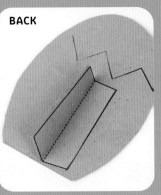

BACK

7 Glue the front of the egg into place along the sides, so that the slider can move freely.

8 Make a stand by folding a rectangle of cardboard in half and gluing it to the back of the egg.

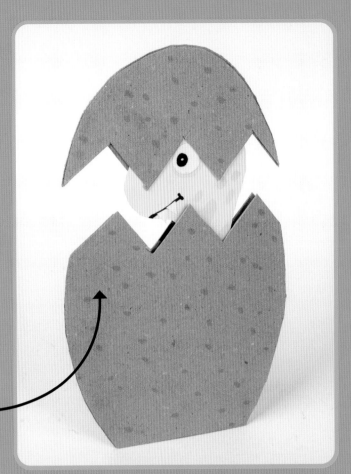

LIFT THE TOP OF THE EGG TO HATCH THE DINOSAUR!

DID YOU KNOW?
Gigantoraptor arranged their eggs in enormous circular nests. They left the middle empty so they could sit on the nest without crushing the eggs.

STEGOSAURUS SKELETON
(STEG-oh-SORE-us)

Stegosaurus is famous for the spiky plates running down the length of its back, and its sharp thagomizer (tail spikes).

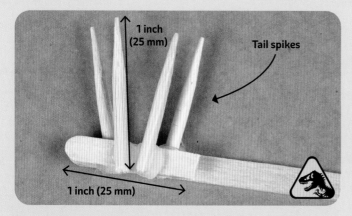

1 inch (25 mm)

1 inch (25 mm)

Tail spikes

1 Cut four spikes from wooden skewer tips, about 1 inch (25 mm) in length. Glue two spikes on each side of the end piece of a coffee stirrer, cut to 1 inch (25 mm).

2 Sandwich the spikes between another two coffee stirrers and glue in place. Trim the stirrers so the tail measures about 2 inches (50 mm) in length.

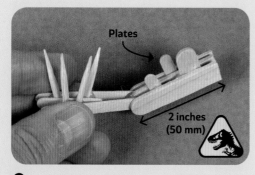

Plates

2 inches (50 mm)

3 Attach the stirrers between the ends of three craft sticks to make the tail. Add vertical pieces of craft stick and stirrer between the sticks to make plates.

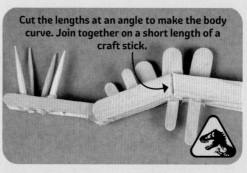

Cut the lengths at an angle to make the body curve. Join together on a short length of a craft stick.

4 Add the next length of spine, adding craft stick plates and coffee stirrer ribs as you do so.

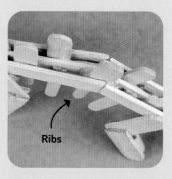

Ribs

5 Work your way along, adding plates and ribs as you go.

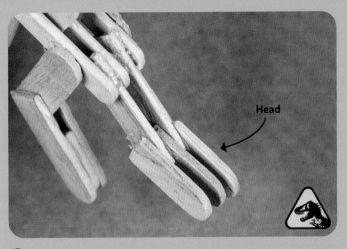

Head

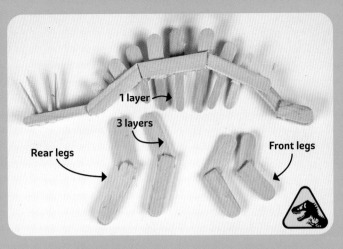

1 layer
3 layers
Rear legs
Front legs

6 Make the neck by sandwiching two pieces of craft stick between the three spine pieces. Then add three identical end pieces for the head.

7 Assemble the legs as shown. The rear legs should be slightly longer than the front legs.

8 Complete the skeleton by gluing the legs on the outside of the body, with the knees bent toward the middle.

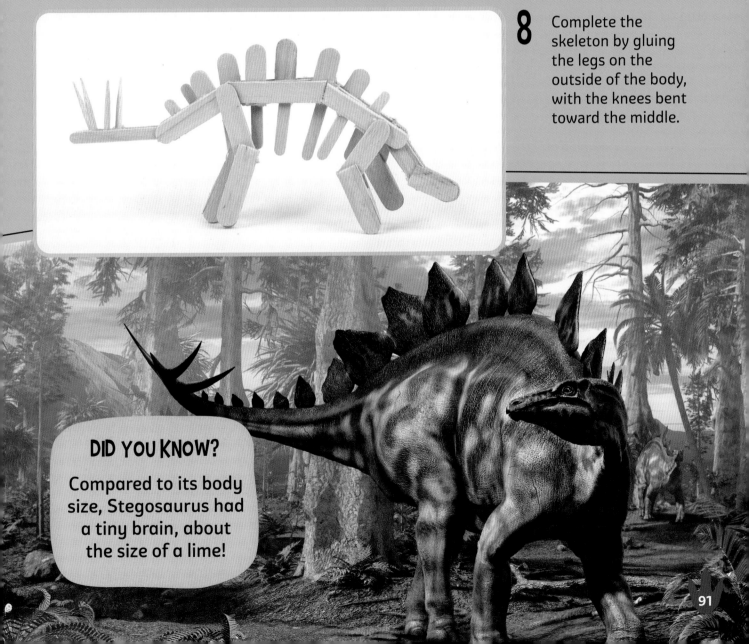

DID YOU KNOW?

Compared to its body size, Stegosaurus had a tiny brain, about the size of a lime!

INDEX

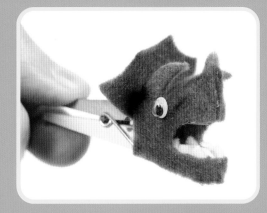

THE AUTHOR

Rob Ives is a UK-based designer and paper engineer. A former teacher, he now specializes in paper animations and science projects, and he often visits schools to talk about design technology and demonstrate his models. His published titles include *Paper Models That Rock!*, *Paper Automata* and the Build it! Make it! series.

PICTURE CREDITS: